# ABSOLUTE ANSWERS

## TO PRODIGAL PROBLEMS

# ABSOLUTE ANSWERS

# TO PRODIGAL PROBLEMS

## EDWIN LOUIS COLE

THOMAS NELSON PUBLISHERS
Nashville

Published in Nashville, Tennessee, by Thomas Nelson, Inc.

Unless otherwise noted Scripture quotations are from the NEW KING JAMES VERSION of the Bible. Copyright © 1979, 1980, 1982, Thomas Nelson, Inc., Publishers

Scripture quotations noted AMPLIFIED BIBLE are from THE AMPLIFIED BIBLE: Old Testament. Copyright © 1962, 1964 by Zondervan Publishing House (used by permission); and from THE AMPLIFIED NEW TESTAMENT. Copyright © 1958 by the Lockman Foundation (used by permission).

Scripture quotations noted TLB are from THE LIVING BIBLE (Wheaton, Illinois: Tyndale House Publishers, 1971) and are used by permission.

Scripture quotations noted KJV are from The Holy Bible, KING JAMES VERSION.

### Library of Congress Cataloging-in-Publication Data

Cole, Edwin Louis.
    Absolute answers to prodigal problems : break through life's barriers forever / Edwin Louis Cole.
        p.    cm.
    Includes bibliographical references.
    ISBN 0-7852-7348-4 (pbk.)
    1. Christian life. I. Title.
BV4501.2.C634    1998
248.4—dc21                                                                98-7201
                                                                              CIP

Printed in the United States of America
3 4 5 6 DHC 03 02 01 00 99

# CONTENTS

# INTRODUCTION
## The Prodigal

There was a man who had two sons. The younger son said, "Father, give me my share of the estate." So the man divided his property between his sons.

Not long after that, the younger son got together all he had, set off for a distant country, and there squandered his wealth in wild living. After he had spent everything, there was a severe famine in that whole country, and he began to be in need. So he hired himself out to a citizen of that country, who sent him to the fields to feed pigs. The son longed to fill his stomach with the pods that the pigs were eating, but no one gave him anything.

When he came to his senses, he said, "How many of my father's hired men have food to spare, and here I am starving to death? I will set out and go back to my father and say to him: Father, I have sinned against heaven and against you. I am no longer worthy to be called your son; make me like one of your hired men."

So he got up and went to his father.

But while he was still a long way off, his father saw him and was filled with compassion for him; he ran to his son, threw his arms around him, and kissed him.

The son said to him, "Father, I have sinned against heaven and against you. I am no longer worthy to be called your son."

But the father said to his servants, "Quick! Bring the best robe and put it on him. Put a ring on his finger and sandals on his feet. Bring the fattened calf and kill it. Let's have a feast and celebrate. For this son of mine was dead and is alive again, he was lost and is found."[1] So they began to celebrate.

# COURAGE

The attitude or response of facing and dealing with anything recognized as dangerous, difficult, painful, instead of withdrawing from it. The quality of being fearless, brave.

Paraphrased from *Webster's Dictionary*

Proverbs 28:1:
The wicked flee when no one pursues,
But the righteous are bold as a lion.

# BOLD

Daring, courageous ... unconventional; showing great liberty of style or expression; standing out to view, striking to the eye.

Paraphrased from *Webster's Dictionary*

One may be fearless where there is no apprehension of danger or no cause for apprehension.... But he is bold only when he is conscious or apprehensive of danger, and prepared to encounter it.

A man may be fearless in a state of inaction; he is bold only in a state of action, or when in a frame of mind for action.

He is intrepid who has no fear when the fearless might tremble.

He is undaunted whose spirit is not discouraged by that which makes the stoutest heart yield.

# CHAPTER ONE
## A Modern Prodigal

I followed my dad's pattern but could not outrun my mother's prayers. I imitated my dad's lifestyle, which put me on a road to devastation, but I became an answer to my mother's prayers.

It seems awkward to start a book talking about things as personal as my relationship with my father, but that relationship illustrates what this book is all about. I was a prodigal. I wandered far from God and the faith of my mother. But, as you'll soon see, the story of the prodigal is the story of all humanity—though not all return to their Father.

Dad's lifestyle was a road to self-destruction;

Mom's pathway led to a long good life, riches, honor, pleasure, and peace.[1]

My dad was the quintessential "hail-fellow-well-met." He never met a stranger. Conviviality was his forte, personal pleasure his love, and work was his passion.

He was a mathematical genius in my eyes. He could add a column of five-digit figures almost as swiftly as an adding machine. He worked in later life in the State and then the Federal Revenue Departments and was always given their most difficult cases. Seldom, if ever, could bookkeepers and accountants hide anything from him. But he was so ingratiating, it took the sting out of the fine if they had to come up with more money.

When he died, more than three hundred men attended his funeral, crowding the chapel. Most of those from both offices where he had worked were there. So were the bookie with whom he placed his bets on the horse races, the news vendor from the corner near where he worked, two waitresses from the restaurant where he ate lunch, as well as many others the family had never met.

He was listed in the telephone directory as E. L.

"King" Cole, the only person at that time listed by his nickname in the Los Angeles phone book, because he was known simply as "King." At times, when I was a young boy and he introduced me to people, Dad would say, "He's just the clown prince." Everyone would laugh but me.

Dad loved sports and would bet on all of them. Mom never knew how much money he really made until he died. When the report came for estate and tax purposes, she was amazed because so much of it had been spent on sports or lost on betting.

I heard the attack on Pearl Harbor announced at a professional football game Dad and I were attending at Gilmore Stadium in Los Angeles. It was only one of the many sports venues we visited, and after he died, I continued to love the sports he taught me. He lived for pleasure of every kind, including alcohol.

We had a troubled household when Dad was drinking and in time I became resentful of it. At times when alcohol was unkind to him, he was unkind to others. Oddly, rather than it driving me to a hatred of alcohol, it did just the opposite. It produced a determination in me to "show him," not by never tasting alcohol, but by developing an ability to do it more and better than he did. One night after receiving a whipping from him that I felt was unfair, I crawled into bed and tearfully vowed that I would out-drink him. That resolution was almost my undoing.

Mom became a Christian years earlier, shortly after they married in Texas. Her sister Ethel had been converted in Los Angeles and wrote the most glowing, intimate, precious letters to my mother of her experience and her love for the Lord. Aunt Ethel cried when she wrote one of them, and her tears stained the pages. Those tearstains were partly responsible for mother attending a tent meeting in Dallas where she, too, was converted.

Not long after that, Mom packed me up, a four-year-old at the time, and we traveled to Los Angeles where she attended a Bible school with her sisters, Ethel and Berta. Dad didn't go with us. It wasn't what he wanted, but Mom went anyway. Since he loved us and Mom wouldn't budge, he eventually joined us.

I missed much of the good part of my high school years due to my preoccupation with learning to drink like Dad. Immediately after graduation, when war broke out, some friends and I enlisted in the United States Coast Guard. Waiting for induction after enlisting, I went to work at the new marine base they were building at Camp Pendleton in southern California. My father was the navy's timekeeper for all personnel on the base.

One evening, Dad invited me to go with him to his friend's house where some fellows were getting together. It was just a group of men from work—a "guy thing"—spending an evening talking and drinking. There was nothing out of the ordinary in that, but it became an extraordinary night for me.

Late that evening, I crossed through the living room of the home we were in, holding a water glass full of whiskey, drinking it straight, when I walked by a couch where my dad was passed out from drinking. I looked at him at that moment and thought, *I won, I outdrank him!* It was a moment of triumph, one I had looked forward to for so long.

Yet, when I continued out the door into the field in front of the house, I looked up into the starry sky and, instead of gloating, I cried, "Is this all there is?" Having reached my goal, such as it was, I felt lonely, desolate, empty, and lost. It was one of the saddest moments of my life.

No exultation of victory. Only a dead, dry defeat.

I was like the prodigal sitting among the pigs in the far country. As I sat down on an old porch chair, I let out a groan—mourning for what had been taken from me by pursuing a dream that had proved to be so worthless. I spent some time that night trying to resolve the disappointment and issues it raised.

Finally, I came to a firm conviction: Mom was right; Dad was wrong. Like the prodigal in the parable, I was finally "coming to myself," realizing the truth.

Not until after the war years, however, would I accept and apply that truth personally. My life then would radically change through Christ's saving grace. My mother's prayers prevailed against my dad's pattern.

God answers prayer!

Mom would live to see me enter the ministry, help support me and my family in those early years, grow to love my wife as her own daughter, and take personal joy in every step of growth God brought us.

But that night, years before, one dream died, and I went years without another to replace it until the Lord put a new dream in my heart. The new dream, birthed by God's Spirit, was to tell everyone I could of the great gift of salvation God gives through Christ.

After a few years in the military, having married while in uniform, I returned home and went to work for a great Christian man, Ralph Calkins, who was like a second father to me. On the job, it was an ever new delight to tell someone of a fresh truth I had learned from Scripture and exhort him to read the Bible, see for himself, and find the most exciting life on earth. Some did. Some didn't.

Because we were near the marine base where I had worked before, off-duty marines would wander around town. I eagerly met them, invited them to a "hospitality home" through our church, had them fed with a good, home-cooked meal, and then told them of God's great love for them.

In those early years, I also went back to preach on the street corner in Los Angeles where Mom had taken me as a boy. She and others would sing, play their instruments, testify, preach, and pray with men who were living on skid row.

My new dream was to share the good news not only with such men, but also with my dad. And I did. I longed to see him love the Lord and for us to be united as a family in faith. I started traveling to see him as often as I could, telling him what God was doing in my life and explaining what a wonderful Savior Jesus was and how satisfied and fulfilled I was now. For four months I carried out this plan.

I wasn't there when it happened, but Mom called and told me when Dad made his commitment to Christ. What a thrill! Then, just four days later, Dad collapsed in Mom's arms from an unsuspected blood clot that had reached his heart. He was gone suddenly, before I had a chance to see him one last time. But it was done, the dream had been realized.

In the almost fifty years since, I've seen hard times, good times, easy times, and tense times. But all those years have been spent serving the Lord. Then came the day in 1995 when I had the opportunity to realize yet another part of the dream God had given me. I was invited to be a guest minister at a Promise Keepers meeting in the Los Angeles Coliseum.

The coliseum isn't far from the home where I grew up, from the places where I had spent my childhood and adolescence, and from Belmont High School where I graduated. Standing on the huge platform at one end of the coliseum, I looked at what was announced to be the largest gathering of Christian men in the world up to that moment. It had been filled when I was there with Dad for various events, but never with men only, and especially with men who were all followers of Christ.

After finishing my teaching, I exercised a moment of pulpit privilege. Boldly, I declared my intention.

Gentlemen, you are seated in a stadium and on a field where I have watched the great Jackie Robinson, Kenny Washington, and Woodrow Strode play football for the University of California at Los Angeles. Where I watched Cotton Warburton, Doyle Nave, and "Antelope" Al Krueger play football for the University of Southern California.

I came here for the Olympic Games with my parents in 1932 and attended them again with my wife in 1984. When the Dodgers moved here from New York, I watched them play their first baseball games in this place. When I took my wife on our first date, I brought her here to watch a football game with me. In all that time, I have seen some great plays and heard some great cheering, but I've never heard this stadium full of men give the greatest cheer possible.

In a moment, I'm going to ask you to stand, and when I count to three, I want you to give the loudest cheer and shout ever heard in this place: We will do it for the Winner of winners, the Champion of all champions—our Lord Jesus Christ!

I counted; they shouted. It was, without a doubt, the greatest and loudest shout ever heard in that place.

Dreams do come true. Only God could take a lonely, empty, lost young man standing in a field in the middle of nowhere and years later put him on a stage in front of more than 72,000 men to lead a shout to the glory of God.

As I write this now, I think of my dad. But it's at my mother's graveside that I stop and thank her for what she meant to my life.

Dad's pattern could not prevail against Mom's prayers. This prodigal came all the way home in more ways than one.

# CHAPTER TWO

## There's More Than One Way to Rebel

The prodigal son wanted to live independently of his father, but rather than doing it in a mature and right manner, he rebelled. A desire to live independently from parents is natural to life. Too often it becomes a negative rather than a positive. Of all the forms of rebellion I believe sedition is one of the worst.

I served on Gary's board of directors. He was, and is, an international minister, and one of my heroes. But a personnel problem developed in his ministry, and eventually it centered on him. Because of the nature of the problem, and the trusted people who were arrayed against him, Gary stepped out of his leadership role for a brief time. Finally, realizing they were wrong and he was right, he stepped back in and began to lead again.

Robert, his devoted vice president, was one of the nicest, friendliest, most helpful people you would want to meet. I was traveling to one of our men's events during their transition, and Robert asked if he could travel with me.

We sat together on the plane, and Robert began to talk about Gary's ministry, what had happened, and what needed to occur now from his perspective. He voiced doubt about the effectiveness of Gary's leadership and wondered if there needed to be a permanent change. He said that so many were now unsure of Gary, that financially there had been a drop-off, and things had not yet fully recovered since Gary's return.

"Who will take his place?" I asked.

"There are several good men who could run things and perhaps do better than Gary at this time," Robert informed me.

"Do you think you could run it?"

"Oh, I'm sure I could, but there are others."

"Would you want to?"

"If it were offered, I would take it, yes."

That smoothie! Robert was setting me up to participate in a seditious plot to unseat Gary. Gary was the visionary, motivator, fund-raiser *par excellence*, and the dynamo that made it all work. And, this was his trusted right arm—a serf, telling me he could take over.

It was all I could do to continue dealing pleasantly with Robert during the trip. I was reminded of King David in the Bible, who had a trusted counselor named Ahithophel who conspired with Absalom, David's son, to take away the kingdom. Absalom broke David's heart. Concerning Ahithophel, David wrote words of pathos and sorrow, tinged with anger about his seditious action: "The words of his mouth were smoother than cream or butter, but war was in his heart; his words were softer than oil, yet they were drawn swords."[1]

In the board meeting that followed a few weeks later, the issue of Gary's continued leadership came to a vote. By that time, I'm sure Robert thought all his votes were set.

Before the vote, we held a discussion on the matter.

"I just have one thing to say," I told the board. "I'm not entering into this act of sedition against Gary, and I want you all to know it."

My words brought a stunned silence. It was out in the open. Immediately, there was a denial of anything subversive. No attempt had been made to oust Gary, his opponents said. How could I think, or especially say, such a thing?

The decision for Gary won by one vote.

To this day, Gary and I are the closest of friends. Those voting against him are long gone. And Gary has done an admirable work around the world.

Sedition is so deceptive and destructive. In America, it's called treason. Those committing it are considered traitors. And those convicted of it can be punished even by death.

*Sedition* is defined as the undermining of constituted authority with the intent to overthrow it.[2] Because it is a work of the flesh, listed as such in Scripture, it is common to life.[3] It creates strife in relationships, causes church splits, topples governments, stifles businesses, leads to divorce, and in its carnal nature is diabolic.

Rebellion by sedition began in heaven when

Lucifer wanted to take the place of God and instead was excommunicated. A place in hell was created for him and all those who followed him in his anarchy against God. Then it continued when Satan led Adam and Eve into rebellion in the Garden of Eden.

Sedition goes on in homes, businesses, and churches all the time. Yet it is seldom, if ever, recognized for the damning thing it is. In corporate America, takeover is the euphemism that gives sedition legitimacy. Employees try to ignore it, husbands and wives are blind to it, criminals engage in it as a matter of policy and procedure, and rebels deny it.

Other forms of rebellion include insubordination, mutiny, and revolt. Each in their own way is disastrous to life. Each of God's prophets had to deal with one or more of these forms of rebellion.

Moses experienced it at the hands of Korah, who enlisted others in an insurrection against his authority. Jealous of Moses' leadership, thinking himself equal in lineage and importance, Korah resented Moses and, in the arrogance of his pride, tried to overthrow him (Num. 16).

Moses showed his character by "falling on his face

before God" and trusting God to vindicate him. God showed Korah's character by having the earth swallow him. Korah's rebellion wasn't against Moses but against the God who appointed and anointed him. No man can fight against God and win.

Indifference is a form of rebellion, as are denial and rejection. Ezekiel experienced it when the people came to hear some new truth, a new song, or some new revelation, but were indifferent to God's Word in application to their lives. They came, they saw, they heard, and paid no attention. Impervious to the personal message, they had no faith that it was from God, that it was to be believed and lived. His message had no righteous result in their lives. Their mutiny against what Jehovah God was saying through His prophet led to captivity and death, the twin fruits of unconcern.

Jeremiah was treated the most harshly by those who begged to know what God was saying in their day—but when they heard it, they refused to believe it was from God because it did not please them. They wanted something different from God, and rejected out of hand what was said.

King David, however, created the rebellion in his son Adonijah's heart through indulging him. David never disciplined him at any time—not so much as a single scolding. A spoiled son, Adonijah in turn tried to spoil his father's kingdom. Adonijah's resentment against his father's failure to recognize him through discipline, which is a sign of caring, degenerated into revolution. Adonijah was eventually put to death for his treason, against not his father but his brother. A warped nature that is unable to be straightened or made "new," will eventually be broken. Those who joined him died with him. "The common bond of rebels is their guilt," says the proverb.[4]

Time after time, the prophets told the people the Word of the Lord, and the people denied that it was of God. The people in turn became prodigal in their lifestyle and ultimately lost what they had hoped to find.

———

The story of the prodigal is not simply a story of a runaway son, but it's your story, my story, and that of all humanity. Great lessons can be learned from the prodigal.

1. *We're all prodigals by nature.* We have turned our back on God our Father, and we need to turn again for home.

2. *Family and friends, and not money, are life's greatest treasure.* When the prodigal's money was gone, so were those who called themselves his friends. When he arrived home broke, destitute, and ravaged by life, he discovered who his true friends were. There's nothing like family.

3. *Maturity brings you back home.* The prodigal left as a boy but returned as a man. He went from demanding, "Give me," to humbly requesting, "Make me." From pride to humility. From hovel to home. From hell to heaven.

4. *Fame can come in a moment, but greatness comes with longevity.* Sure, he was popular, but only for a short while.

5. *Time is not measured by years alone, but by inner experiences.* Aging can occur in a night, in an instant. Some years ago, my friend Don Ostrom and I were talking about a mutual friend, whose refusal to accept counsel and advice in his older years caused him to leave his business to the wrong son. The result was disastrous. "Better a poor and wise youth

than an old and foolish king who will be admonished no more," is the scriptural truth.[5]

6. *Influence is a commodity in life that is wise to use, but criminal to sell.*

7. *Distance is measured not by miles, but by affection.* Two people can share the same name, live in the same home, lie in the same bed, and be miles apart.

8. *Men and nations are not great by virtue of their wealth, but by the wealth of their virtues.*

9. *Man's greatness is not found in his physical prowess, reputation, or position of power; it is found in his care for others.* "Your care for others is the measure of your greatness," is how Jesus said it.[6]

The prodigal wasted the best years of his life on himself, but when he returned home, none despised him. Instead, they welcomed him with open arms, warm hearts, genuine joy, instant forgiveness, and grace without bounds. In it all he learned one of life's greatest lessons: that love for God is not based on the depth of sin in one's life when forgiven, but on the depth of the knowledge of forgiveness of sin.[7]

Little forgiven, little love. Much forgiven, much love. The prodigal learned his lesson.

The best news in the parable of the prodigal is that when the wayward, rebellious son finally came home, the heroic father did not rail against him but celebrated the return of the son he loved and had waited for all that time. The son was willing to accept a lower level of life—that of a servant—but the father wouldn't hear of it and restored him to his place of sonship.

We're all prodigals at best when we're without God—doing our own thing our own way, without giving thought to Him or His will. Gripped by spiritual vertigo, we think we are rising higher and higher in life, only to find we've lost our sense of direction and are actually heading for a crash and destruction.

Jesus said the prodigal eventually "came to himself"—evidence that he wasn't thinking right when he was running from his father. All of us without God are exactly like that. We are unable to think properly because we're running from our heavenly Father who created us and waits for us to come to our senses and return to Him.

We believe our reasons are good for running, because we feel so guilty about what we've done, where we've wound up, and what a quandary we find ourselves in—inextricably mired in it and yet ever struggling to get out. Yet, all we have to do is admit we've come short of our Father's glory and ask for His forgiveness, and we will receive it. He did it for the prodigal. He did it for me. And, He will do the same for you.

# CHAPTER THREE
## Adult Adolescence

When Adam sinned in the Garden of Eden, he set a pattern that humans have followed ever since.

God's commandment was to enjoy every tree in the garden except the tree of the knowledge of good and evil. That one Adam and Eve were not to touch. In the day that Adam took the forbidden fruit, he denied God's right of possession, His sovereignty, and sinned against Him.

When God wanted Adam to accept responsibility for his actions, he refused. "The woman whom You gave to be with me, she gave me of the tree, and

I ate," he retorted.[1] In that moment, Adam refused to accept responsibility for his own actions, and in so doing, he lost the manhood God had given him. In the vernacular of our day, it's called *denial.*

The pattern that Adam established in the garden is: deception, denial, distraction, dislocation, and destruction. Adam was deceived into thinking the fruit and the knowledge it offered were better than relationship with God. When caught, he denied his guilt. He was distracted to the point that he tried to hide from the God who made him. Then he was dislocated from the garden God had provided. And, in the instant he sinned, destruction came in the form of spiritual death.

Another example of this is the adulterer, who is deceived into thinking no one will know, denies doing anything wrong, is distracted in mind by the illicit, is dislocated physically by going where he shouldn't, and eventually destroys the marital relationship. Men are deceived into destruction all the time. Take for example a young Connecticut man I'll call Scott.

Scott's wife sensed there was a problem with their marriage. She called me to ask if I would talk to him.

It was something I knew I needed to do, so I made time and found a place for it.

"What's going on?" I asked.

"Nothing," he replied. "Why do you ask?"

"I want to help, but first I need to know," I said.

"I don't need any help. Everything's fine. There isn't anything I can't handle."

"What is it you're trying to handle?" I asked.

"Nothing!"

But there was, and eventually he told me he was taking a "little" cocaine.

Deceived into thinking he could handle it, denying anything was wrong, distracted from his work, dislocated from home after work, Scott's actions were leading to the destruction of his marriage.

Admitting the truth is the first step in recovery. Denial is a barrier that prohibits cures, healing, help, and salvation of every kind. "You can't heal a wound by saying it's not there!" is how Jeremiah phrased it.[2] Scott's refusal to accept responsibility for his actions was causing him to lose authority at work and influence at home.

With Scott's knowledge, I told his wife what the problem was. She said, "Thank God." Knowing what the problem was, having it out in the open, relieved her to deal with it. The truth set her free from the bondage of the fear of the unknown. Now she could take some action and try to get help for Scott.

Deception leads to destruction. Unbelief is the basis of sin, pride is the strength of sin, and deceitfulness is the character of sin. Pride is sin's strength because it will not allow us to humble ourselves to admit need, ask for help, or seek a change. It imprisons men.

Devilish power is always deceptive to entice us into the bondage of addiction. *All sin promises to serve and to please but only desires to enslave and to dominate.* The perversion of our world is never more clearly seen than when you realize God gave dominion over plants to men, but today plants are taking dominion over men. Alcohol, cigarettes, marijuana, and cocaine are all made from plants. They reduce men to a level not only below that of animals, but even that of vegetation.

Independence is a natural desire, a mark of manhood, but it can also be either a vice or a virtue, or a force for rebellion. The prodigal rebelled. He no longer wanted to live by his father's standards or under his mother's supervision, but free from parental guidance. Taking his inheritance from his father, the prodigal went into a far country to live his own way, and his way was degenerative. It led him into a level of life lower than the animals. The pigs in the sty where he was had it better than he did—they had the pea, he had the pod.

He could have learned life's lessons from observation at home rather than experience them in an insane manner. *All sin is a form of insanity*, the ultimate end of which is death.

Finally, accepting responsibility for his actions, humbly turning toward home, he was returned by his father's grace to his rightful position of sonship.

The pattern of the prodigal is rebellion, ruin, repentance, reconciliation, and restoration. Repentance is the pivotal point between ruin and reconciliation. That's true not only in the parable, but in society as a whole, as well as in an individual life.

Accepting responsibility, being a man, doing what is right, turning it around, coming home—say it any way you will—it all means that every man needs to come into his right mind and come home to God the Father so he can be restored to the place of sonship.

Not only God, but women want men to be men too. I was in Seattle, and a group of us who where attending a men's event took a freight elevator to another floor. A woman who was dressed in a security uniform operated it.

"What do you think about our men's meeting?" I asked her.

"I'm tired of men's femininity," she said firmly.

Those with me glanced her way, and I wondered aloud to her why she felt that way.

"Look," she began. "I'm the chief of security in this building today. I'm a woman. This is a man's job. You want to know why they don't have it?"

"Please tell me."

"Because the men call me to make a decision for them that they should be able to make. They won't do it—don't want to take the responsibility. So, here I am, their supervisor."

We left the elevator discussing her indictment of men. The pattern of men refusing to accept responsibility continues. "They became like women," the prophet said about the men of Babylon.[3] "They have forborne to fight."[4] They wouldn't take a stand.

The men in that chief security officer's company wouldn't take responsibility, so she became a supervisor by default. She had to make decisions for them when they would not. That's what a mother does for her children. Those men were acting like children and forcing her to act like their mother. It happens in marriages as well: *When a man acts like a child it forces his wife to act like his mother.*

In the great transition chapter in the Bible, the key verse for transition is this: "When I was a child, I spoke as a child, I understood as a child, I thought as a child; but when I became a man, I put away childish things."[5]

The truth is there for all to see. Christians are to grow up as mature people able to speak God's Word, understand His truths, and think His thoughts from His Word. But, there are other aspects of it as well. Just as the elevator operator had to "mother" the men with whom she worked, so many wives end up mothering their husbands.

Mothers do two things for their children: correct them and make decisions for them. They do the same with men who are childish.

Here are seven characteristics of a child:

1. Is the center of his own universe.
2. Is insensitive to others' needs.
3. Demands his own way.
4. Throws a temper tantrum if he's not catered to.
5. Is irresponsible in behavior.
6. Is unreasonable.
7. Is subject only to concrete authority.

Grown men can act very childish. Look at the headlines every day.

- A sports strike reaches an impasse when neither players nor owners want to accept the other's terms—childish attitudes with dire consequences. They finally agree to play ball when subjected to concrete authority by a government arbitrator, but with nothing settled.
- Men from two warring factions sit down at a table to iron out a peace treaty. When a leader of one of the factions sees that the others will not "play by his rules," he leaves, and the war rages on.

Jesus said the men of this generation are like children playing in the marketplace. When others won't play their game with them their way, they get up and leave.[6] "Either play by my rules, or I won't play," is a childish philosophy.

The natural maturation process in life is *supposed* to be ongoing. From birth to around the age of four, children are helped to mature through "concrete authority," often expressed by the phrase, "Because I said so."

That changes in adolescence. The "rod" of concrete authority changes to "understanding." The rod is like a ruler with lines drawn on it to show the limits of acceptable behavior. The lines help young people know the difference between right and wrong and how far they can go before reaching the boundaries of good behavior.

Lines are drawn all through life, but adolescence is the developing, understanding age in maturity. Such lines are drawn between passing and failing in school. Those failing might not appreciate it, but they knew the line was there just the same. The same is true between a misdemeanor and a felony in law. A dollar may be the only distance between them— steal one dollar more and the crime jumps into a more serious category. Or a day: One day after your eighteenth birthday, you go to jail. The lines are drawn. Cross the line, and you suffer the consequences.

Lines are also drawn in the street to keep drivers from killing themselves. Cross the line, and you might die in an accident. The lines aren't there to keep you from having a good time, but to keep you from killing yourself.

As a child grows into and through the teen years, the idea is for him to learn principles upon which to build a life. Life is lived by principles or laws (elemental, moral, physical, natural). They're given to enable us to have and enjoy life. The more we live by principle, the straighter our course will be.

After the age of about twenty-five, if a man has not learned how to live by the measurements of behavior—to be reasoned with and guided by principles—he has to be dealt with again, as in childhood, by concrete authority.

Today in America, the lines of behavior are being obliterated by those who want no limits on their conduct. The resulting confusion is creating havoc in America's schools, tragedies in families, and even death for many young people.

## Adult Adolescence

Baseball players are banned "for life" for substance abuse, then reinstated time after time, which destroys all deterrent effect for penalties. Young people laugh at laws. They regard them as meaningless. Older people who make the laws and then disregard them are viewed with disdain by all.

Millions of men today did not mature properly. They never learned the lines of proper behavior, they ignored principles and laws, they refused to accept responsibility for their antisocial acts, and they're in prison because they must be dealt with by concrete authority. Many of them, when discharged, order their steps in the same old pattern and suffer once again at the hands of the police and the courts.

Because of the childishness rampant in men, the world is in chaos, and only such concrete authorities as divorce courts, foreclosures, and prisons, among others, cause men to submit to authority.

The phone in my hotel room rang one night when I was in a distant city for a men's event. A female voice said, "Mr. Cole, my husband is coming to your meeting tomorrow, and our marriage is in trouble, but he won't listen to me. I want to get help; he says he doesn't need it. But we really do. Could you talk to him?" When I asked why he wouldn't seek help, she replied, "Because he is a pastor." I told her I didn't know what could be done under such circumstances but that I would pray that her husband would pay attention to the message. He didn't.

Today he refuses to discuss the issues, will not admit he has a need, doesn't understand her complaint, and as a result, has submitted to the concrete authority of a judge in divorce court.

Divorce courts are full of childish people, both men and women, who will probably be cursed to repeat their failure with someone else unless they grow up.

A man acting like a child, forcing his wife to act as his mother, has another real problem: You can't make love to your mother.

As a result of the impediment he feels in the sexual relationship, her husband begins to find surrogate satisfaction with pornography, habitual masturbation, sexual videos, or even an extramarital affair. And he blames his wife. But if he's in an illicit relationship and leaves his wife, it's only a matter of time after being with his lover full-time that he acts like a child, and she acts like his mother, their sex life dwindles, and he's blaming her. It's a vicious circle, and it's being repeated time after time in today's society.

Let me make one distinction, however. There is a world of difference between being childlike and being childish. Our Lord actually commended children and said men needed to be like them in certain ways: "In malice be ye children, but in understanding be men."[7] But childishness in men is deplorable.

Here's a letter I received from a man who learned this distinction:

Words can't cover the flood of overflowing love of Jesus I'm feeling; the blood of the Lamb means something to me now. I work for a psychic phone line in my home. I started to notice I wasn't helping myself, my family, or the people on the other end of the phone.... These folks are paying $2.00 to $4.00 per minute to talk to a stranger about their past and the future. I won't be a part of it any longer. I, for one, have come home and am giving my clients my testimony and witness for the Lord with another past psychic that has come home also. We'll no longer teach that silly psychic doctrine to anyone, nor will we remember it. I formerly tried to tell my children's future from the stars, but now I don't because I've met the One who made the stars. Dr. Cole, I helped more people in four days using your "Take Responsibility" tape than all the peeping and muttering I was using. Guide, guard, govern . . . denial, distortion, destruction . . . the lighter yoke of Jesus has worked miracles for my young callers. I love the Lord, I love everyone. A child who became a man at 49.

He signed it, "A child at 49." He at last had put away childish things, became childlike, and through it, became a man. Paradox of paradoxes.

In your relationships with God, your wife, your children, your church, your work, your leisure activities—are you acting like a man? Are you accepting responsibility for your actions, admitting need, repenting of wrong, believing God's love for you, receiving His forgiveness, and rejoicing in being restored to His family? Or are you childish, trying like Adam to live in denial?

# CHAPTER FOUR

## If They Can Make It, So Can You

You're only young once, but you can live immaturely for a lifetime.

Before a man is anything else—husband, father, businessman—he's a man, and what he is in his manhood determines what he is in every other aspect of his life. So when a man changes, the world changes because his manhood affects all his other actions. Change is the only constant in maturity. Positive change *is* possible.

I received a letter from a man who wrote of the change in his life when he began to accept responsibility for his actions, and how it affected him. "Dear Ed," he wrote,

> I have followed your ministry for nine years. I've lost my job in the field I studied for. I've lost my wife after thirteen years of marriage. I've lost my children, home, cars, livelihood. But, I haven't lost the essence of who you are and what your ministry represents in my life.
>
> Through seven of those nine years, I thought you were too tough—too rigid—too antiquated in your ideals. I would do it my way! And so, I did. Ed Cole was a "hard guy." Maximized Manhood was for "weak sissies" who couldn't suck it up and take ownership of their circumstances.
>
> You once graciously spoke to me at a meeting in Boulder, Colorado, and gave me one of your books—for free! That was the highlight of my trip. I kept saying, "Ed Cole, the hard guy, stopped and talked to me."
>
> My "dark side" reads like this: dirty magazines my wife would find, adultery, X-rated videos, poor financial management, my word meaning nothing. I'd blame our lousy sex life on her. But, now I am a

changed man. Why did it take me so long to hear the truth, when I heard the message? When you said recently, "Truth is confrontational and controversial," I wanted to jump for joy. Because I am now a witness to the precepts of living in truth every day.

This is not a pity party I've posed to you. But, I want you to know I'm living the life of a real man. At last, I've become a man. I've accepted responsibility for my actions, asked God to forgive me, and He has, and, at last, I've grown up.

This man had heard the Word many times, but when he became a "doer" of the Word, his life changed. The prodigal finally came home, and the Father forgave him, reconciled him unto Himself, and restored him to a right relationship. The process of restoration is under way with the rest of his life.

Isn't it amazing that a man can attend church, be around the gospel, attend men's meetings, buy the books, and never have it touch his life? That's why one of the lessons of the prodigal is that *distance is not always measured by miles but by affection.* You can hear the truth, yet be miles away because you don't love truth. Yet when the prodigal accepted the truth, that his dad was right, the distance between him and his dad instantly closed.

Sitting in those meetings, the man who wrote me that letter was millions of miles from God because a love for God was missing in his life. But a simple act of genuine repentance changed his life from ruin to reconciliation. It's God's pattern and His glory.

The Christian Men's Network holds what we call "Summit" meetings over a period of three days for in-depth teaching to men. On Saturday, there's an informal program in which we award certificates to those who have completed the course.

We used to give each attendee one minute after receiving his certificate to tell what benefit the meetings had been to him. The time limit represented a challenge to them, and almost without exception they had to write out what they wanted to say and read it to the audience. We would hoot, holler, slap high fives, and have a great time.

One of the classic speeches occurred after I had spent four sessions teaching truths concerning men's childishness and how it forces the wife to act like a mother. The line "You can't make love to your mother" really got to an attendee named Bill. When his turn came to speak, he didn't need to read anything. He just stood in front of the microphone and said simply, "Hello wife, good-bye Mom." Every man howled with laughter. We all identified with it.

No matter how it's done, it must be done: Recognition of a prodigal problem is vital to a man and his manhood. I received a letter a month or two before a return visit to a city for another men's event. A man who had attended the last meeting wrote me and shared his life so openly and truthfully that I respected him, though I'd never met him. During the course of the event, I read his letter publicly and asked if he was present. When he strode up on the stage, the men stood and cheered him. This is what he had written:

> Dear Ed, I'm writing to let you know that I am a man, sixty years old, and at the time I saw you last year, I had been an elder in my church for thirteen years. I had traveled overseas with ministries, but I came to your meeting as an adulterer. I had been in that relationship for twenty years. The Word that day pricked my heart, but I wasn't man enough to admit it as I saw hundreds of others do.

A month after your meeting, I had a heart attack. My wife of thirty-seven years confronted me after finding a card I had received from the woman (who was married). I confessed everything to her. I told my pastor, stepped down as an elder, and submitted myself to my pastor and elders for repentance, recovery, and restoration to the Lord and the church. It was too much for my wife, and she divorced me.

I've asked God to forgive me, and I'm sure He has. My children have. But I know I have to walk it out. I've read and reread *Maximized Manhood* so many times. I'm looking forward to being with you at the event, and I'm coming as a different man!

My pastor has stuck with me and my wife. I thank him for that. He has helped to give me the accountability I needed. Please understand it was easy to write this because I am not afraid anymore. Whatever God requires of me, I'm ready.

The prodigal came home. For twenty years he lived in deception, denying anything was wrong, distracted by the relationship, dislocated from his wife and family, and headed for destruction.

Without God's love, mercy, and forgiveness, he would not be the man he is today. He came to himself and came back to his heavenly Father, and his honesty caused other men to appreciate him.

Only God can make that kind of change in a man's life.

God didn't condemn him for his actions; his sin condemned him. When he came home to the Father, he was reconciled and restored to his rightful place. What a great God! Not all of us must make it so public, but we must all do it.

When you're born to be a man, becoming one is the greatest thing in the world. Are you a male or a man? Every one of us must make the choice.

Take heart from the examples of men in this chapter and choose the manhood of Christlikeness.

# CHAPTER FIVE

## Fatherlessness

A number of years ago, Ben Kinchlow wrote that while being a male is a matter of birth, being a man is a matter of choice.[1] I challenge you to make that choice. When a prodigal man makes the choice, he has a Father waiting to greet him who frees him from any void in his life.

As I said earlier, the lines marking the limits of acceptable behavior are being erased at an ever increasing pace, resulting in confusion that reigns in families, homes, and the world at large. We're in a time of great transition. So much is happening so fast that it seems to create stress, confusion, and fear in the hearts and lives of everyone.

The need to declare a standard for manhood is ever present, yet too much of it is being done by psychologists analyzing rather than prophets declaring. There's a vast difference between a word that is inspirational and informational and one that is instructional and prophetically confrontational.

Dale Carnegie, in his classic book *How to Win Friends and Influence People*, said that in his research over a period of years, he learned not to try to compel people to admit they were wrong. It's an almost impossible task. In some cultures, "saving face" is even more important than life itself. People would rather die than lose face. So, to succeed with people, Carnegie said, you need to give them ways to change without their having to admit they're wrong.[2]

God, however, doesn't take that approach. Entrance into His kingdom is not based on meritorious accomplishment, nor did Christ allow men to save face by circumventing the need to repent. Repentance is still the pivotal point between death and life—eternal life, that is.

All of us, without God, are prodigals to one extent

or another. Yet people—men especially—have a hard time admitting that. Men seem to think they can find their own way and fight their way through anything. Even when they lose their way, they are too proud to admit it. It's a stereotype, yet it is true that many men are too proud even to ask for road directions.

Many men would rather believe a lie than admit the truth when confronted with it, still trying to cover themselves with fig-leaf alibis, excuses, and blaming others rather than facing the reality of truth. They would rather spend more time denying the truth than save time by admitting to it, because that would force them to admit they were wrong. The modern-day legal profession has made a science of teaching men to "stonewall," to refuse to acknowledge or admit any wrong they did or might have done. That stone wall imprisons them in the lie.

For the Christian, repentance is a way of life, something—given the power of the fleshly nature of our lives—that we practice to maintain rightness before God. Repentance is not a work to be performed. We're not saved *for* repenting, but *if* we repent. It means turning from evil and embracing by faith that which is righteous.

Jesus said that even someone coming back from the dead could not bring to repentance someone who rejects the truth of the gospel.[3] His own miracles left the towns of Chorazin and Bethsaida unmoved spiritually, and he said it would be better for Sodom and Gomorrah than for them in the judgment.[4]

Repentance comes when we, like the prodigal, "come to our senses," recognize our sin, and want to be free of its power over us—its consequences, guilt, condemnation, addictions, disease, and whatever else it has brought to our lives.

For me, a few years after I recognized the rightness of my mother's faith, I could no longer stand the thought of being without God. The sheer misery that knowledge produced in my life brought me to my knees. Absence from God was a terror to me. I knew it was the reason for the misery I was causing others, and I could no longer bluff my way around it. I simply needed God, and that was that.

So, whatever it took to have the presence of God in my life, if it meant giving up everything in my life—I wanted God! Knowing Him means more to me than life itself. So, when I say something, do something, or act in some way displeasing to God, repentance is the way back home. That truth has never changed.

But there's even more to it than just repentance, because beyond forgiveness there is cleansing. "If we confess our sins He is faithful and just to forgive us our sins, and to cleanse us from all unrighteousness."[5]

When the prodigal returned, the father took him back into his home, put the best robe on him, and gave him sandals and a signet ring marking his position of authority as a son of the master. The young man's rebellion was put behind them and forgotten. The prodigal was a prodigal no more, but a son enjoying the full love of his father and all the privileges of being an heir to the estate. Relationships were restored. He was forgiven of his sin and cleansed from his past. That cleansing also took care of habits he had learned while away from his father.

George Fitzgerald is now a missionary minister to the prisons of this world. He spent twenty-one years on drugs and thirteen in prison. He has the perfect answer for those who bring up his past about being an ex-con or ex–drug addict.

"I'm not an ex-anything," George says. "I am a new creation in Christ Jesus."

He grew up on the streets of Brooklyn, New York, without a father to help or guide him. He learned about life from the streets, became streetwise, and, as he sought acceptance, identity, discipline, love, and value, spent time with various groups, gangs, and religious people. But when he turned to God in genuine, heartfelt repentance, his life changed.

George is one of what is now being called a "fatherless generation." I wrote in *Maximized Manhood* in 1982, "The absentee father is the curse of our day."[6] In the intervening years, the situation has only grown worse. No longer subject merely to absentees, we are now cursed with a growing void. *Fatherlessness* describes the present societal condition. It suggests an impending disaster, a cataclysmic catastrophe in the making. History teaches what fatherlessness can do to a society.

After World War I, Germany became known as a "fatherless nation." So many dads died in the war that the youth had few fathers, role models, or disciplinarians. Without fathers, those children were without a heritage. The significance of this can be seen in a statement by Lenin: "Take away the heritage of a people and they are easily persuaded."[7]

In the absence of fathers to guide them, the German youths gathered among themselves to find comfort and strength. Beer halls were popular places to hang out, cuss, and discuss the issues of the day. It was there that they heard a new philosophy and the hope it offered.

Originally Nazis held traditional values of family, home, and country. The promoter and preacher of this new order began to call Germany "the Fatherland." It gave an identity in a culture where there was no father with which to identify. The fatherless embraced the new philosophy.

Adolf Hitler united the people with the persuasion of a better society that would bring about a new Germany, with every man working for a greater good. Hitler promised to reinvent government. Government could and would provide the solution to the ills of the country. His philosophy was based on the concept of "equalizing the gears," which is similar to the "political correctness" doctrine of today.

The frustration with the established government

felt by fatherless youth led to anger, a loss of trust in the truthfulness of its leaders, and the formation of groups embracing myths about it. In the new philosophy was an antigovernment subtlety, appealing to the youth against the old civic leaders. An emphasis on youth is common to revolutions. The young are eager to serve, while they think the older generation is interested only in money or status quo. As a result, antigovernment feelings steadily grew more strident and were openly sanctioned.

After Hitler came to power he declared his party to be the "Nationalist Socialistic Party." By then, the youth were organized, and many in the church who had been seduced and deceived by Hitler's original message realized they had been betrayed. The rest, as they say, is history—the history of a fatherless generation.

After World War II, the Soviet Union also became known as a fatherless nation. Of every 1,000 men who went to war, only 17 came home, and only 3 came home *not* wounded, maimed, or crippled. The young were bereft of a father's leadership, counsel, and mentoring. Again, in a way similar to the pre–World War II German experience, a message was sounded to which many of the youths responded.

"Capture the youth, and you capture the nation," was the communist dictum. The Bolsheviks called themselves "dead men on furlough." The communists appealed to the hopelessness of youth and promised a beneficial destiny. Life was expendable during the war and after the war, and remained expendable in civilian life.

Today, not through a physical war, but a moral war, the United States is being classified as a nation of the fatherless. A conference that was held regarding the rise of crime in the nation concluded that its number one cause is the breakdown of the family, and the number one cause for the breakdown of the family is fatherlessness.[8] In light of what has happened to fatherless nations in the past, what does the future hold?

Back then, the younger generation felt alienated from the older, isolated from government, and suspicious of their leaders. A new group arose wanting freedom but practicing totalitarianism. They weren't called "gangs" then, but "thugs." Nor were they called "militia," but they became storm troopers and Reds.

Morality was abandoned as a societal more. Does that description sound familiar?

A poll taken by *Time* magazine asked people to identify the main problem facing America. Crime, said 25 percent of the respondents. Fifteen percent said drugs; 11 percent cited unemployment; another 11 percent said the economy; 8 percent said racism; and 6 percent said morals.[9] Morality was largely abandoned as a concern. Morality is no longer considered foundational to this nation and its people.

God is providing a solution for the loss of morality brought on by our society's fatherlessness, just as He has met mankind's needs since the Garden of Eden. That solution is the current men's movement, which is turning the hearts of the fathers to their children, and the children to their fathers. Scripture says God would do that lest He come and strike the earth with a curse.[10]

God has raised up a modern-day men's movement to prevent the same thing from happening today that happened with previous generations. It is our only hope.

Now it's time for each of us to repent and accept the responsibility God created for us to exercise, including that of being strong fathers—lest we follow the same old pattern as other nations have with previous generations. God forbid!

Beyond forgiveness there is cleansing, meaning complete freedom. Freedom from the curse of fatherlessness. Freedom from a lack of direction, from hopelessness, from a void in your life. No longer an ex-anything, you can be a whole man.

# CHAPTER SIX

## Think, Act, Then Feel

For a long time, I've emphasized the truth that real men *think* before they *act*. How else can we act responsibly? But, just because it's true and I teach it doesn't mean I'm always able to live it.

I spoke once on this very subject to a large gathering in Chicago. "Children," I said, "follow a process of feeling, acting, and then thinking while mature men practice thinking, acting, and finally feeling." The audience responded positively to the message, and it was a good night overall.

The next day, I was due to fly from Chicago back to my home. Sitting in a hotel room that Saturday morning, it suddenly occurred to me that I didn't have to wait the five hours before my scheduled flight would leave because I could catch the earlier plane. After calling and changing my flight plans, I hurriedly packed, dressed, and rushed by taxi to the airport.

While exchanging my ticket for the earlier flight, a sudden picture flashed into my mind of the honorarium check lying on the dresser in my hotel room. I felt an emotional rush as I thought about the maid cleaning my room and finding the check.

Quickly leaving the airline counter with my new ticket, I hurried outside for a taxi to return me to the hotel. It was an hour-long ride, but nothing seemed to matter except getting back to that room.

Bursting into the room I had left just two hours before, I scanned the dresser for the check. Not there! Could I have taken it and not known it? I emptied my briefcase and computer case, then checked my luggage—nothing.

Thoughts flooded my mind of calling hotel security, informing the manager, finding the maid (except she hadn't been in the room to clean it yet)—doing anything and doing it quickly. Then I decided to unzip my garment bag once again and search through the pockets of the suit I had worn the night before. No check.

Just before calling security, I sat on the bed and retraced my steps after entering the room the previous night. I knew I had put that check on the dresser, and I wondered what could have happened to it. Then, and only then, after I had collected myself and really thought about it all, did I decide to look in the pocket of the *shirt* I had worn the night before.

And there it was.

Sitting on the side of the bed, thinking of my foolishness, of how silly I had been acting, my own words echoed in my mind that real men *think,* act, and then feel. I felt so foolish, immature, thoughtless—so adolescent—not at all like the man standing before the audience proclaiming truth to them. Oh, I was so glad no one was traveling with me and knew what I had done. Of course, now, I'll probably never hear the end of it! God keeps us humble.

I use my story to illustrate the truth that we can act like men one minute and act childishly the next, as we act without thinking. The night before, I was a man, and two thousand people listened and heeded my counsel. The following morning, I reacted to what I *felt* before I *thought* and had to laugh at my own childishness later.

Meditation is often considered the domain of Eastern gurus, but actually meditation is the womb of creativity. When I at last sat down to think the situation through, to meditate, creative thinking brought me the solution to my dilemma.

Consequences follow actions. Those who act childishly don't think of the results, only the pleasure at the time. Pleasure lasts for a brief moment, but the consequences can last for a lifetime or an eternity.

"I quit my job. They weren't paying enough. I can do a lot better than work in that place." With those words, Chuck informed Harold, his father-in-law, of a change he was making. Harold was concerned. This was Chuck's sixth job change in five years of marriage, and each time Harold had helped his daughter's family financially.

"But what will you do for income until you find something else?" Harold asked.

"I'll find something, don't worry," Chuck answered.

## Think, Act, Then Feel

Throughout that day, as Harold thought about it, his thoughts were unkind toward Chuck. Harold fretted, not realizing the exhortation in Scripture: "Fret not thyself because of evildoers."[1] To Harold, Chuck was an evildoer in that he wasn't providing for his own. Scripture says that if you don't do that, you're worse than an infidel.[2] Harold's instability caused a hardship on the entire family.

Reacting without thought of consequence is a mark of immaturity and irresponsibility. And that's exactly what Chuck was doing, quickly leaving a job when something happened that he didn't like, giving no thought to what he would do next or how he would meet his family's needs in the meantime.

For those thinking it is faith to act without regard for consequences, they had better make sure they have the Word of God to stand on, because the Word is the substance of faith. You can walk on the Word, not on feelings or presumption.

A fatherless generation naturally has a "father hunger," but it must be fed from the source from which all healing comes. Without the Bible, the knowledge of how to obtain the manhood of Jesus Christ is missing.

Unfortunately, much of our world is in the grip of a new psychology that says that feeling is more important than thinking. As you read your newspaper, you'll see that the words *I feel* are replacing *I think* in Washington, D.C., discourses. The result of the ascendancy of feeling over thought is a nation and world of grown-up boys who rarely become mature in masculinity. The old Peter Pan syndrome is still operative.

Consider the childishness of men in prison who suffer incarceration, generally as a result of acting before thinking, letting their feelings dictate their actions. A high percentage of imprisoned men are there as a result of temper tantrums. Tantrums are childish, and in grown men, they're disastrous.

Moses, a godly leader, had a tantrum when God told him to touch the rock. In his frustration with Israel, instead of touching it, Moses struck it twice, and God would not let him enter Canaan, the land of promise. Moses spent forty years in the back side of the desert, where God tempered, tamed, and tried him. But one angry act, just one, kept him out of Canaan.

Men who abuse women generally do it when they

are having a temper tantrum. Sure, there are devils that stir men up, but consider that the vast majority of abusers are just men who have never matured. They never learned to reason, so they've always solved their problems with violence. It's a learned behavior from childhood.

In Brazil years ago, I heard a story I've never forgotten, because the moral is so filled with truth. It seems a man spent a lifetime in a little, backward town trying to make a watch out of straw. In his later years, he finally accomplished it.

Because it was such an incredible scientific breakthrough, the world wanted to visit and see it. So a day was set for people from all over to come, and the town was readied for company.

The little town square was mobbed. On a table near the dais, waiting for the demonstration ceremony, the watch was laid. Everyone was enjoying a moment of conviviality before the big event.

Meanwhile, wandering down from the hills came an old burro that sauntered nonchalantly through the crowd. No one paid him any attention. As he neared the table, he spotted the watch, and in one gulp it was gone.

The moral of the story is that one jackass stunt can ruin a lifetime of work.

It's the same with every man—there's a burro in all of us.

Millions of men have lost everything because they acted in one foolish moment before they stopped to think. But mature men put away childish things. They think before they act.

We may all fail at times, but we begin to recover by putting away childish things and showing ourselves to be men.

———

With responsibility comes accountability. When I was trustee of my mother's will, her entire estate was under my stewardship. My moral responsibilities were to her, then I had legal obligations to the state, and finally an ethical duty to her heirs. There was an accountability to each of them, but most of all an accountability to God for my stewardship and integrity. Legality, morality, ethics, and spirituality are the criteria for decision making.

So it is with you and Christ's "trust." The apostle Paul said he was put "in trust" with the gospel of Jesus Christ. God trusted him with His Word, anointing, gifts, and calling to accomplish His purpose on earth. That was Paul's responsibility. And with it came accountability: "Woe is me if I do not preach the gospel!" he said.[3]

Think about God's putting confidence in you—His committing to your care the very truth that makes a difference between hell and heaven to those who hear and believe. "Go therefore and make disciples," Jesus commanded all His followers.[4] The gospel is in your trust. Your family is in your trust, too. Your talents, your job, your friendships—you're a trustee, a steward of them all. As such, you will give an account of yourself to God.

In a nation like America, democracy is a trust as well. To have the right to vote and not vote is a violation of that trust—especially when one vote can affect the nation or the world:

- In 1645, one vote gave Oliver Cromwell control of England.
- In 1649, one vote caused Charles I to be executed.
- In 1776, one vote gave America the English language instead of German.

- In 1845, one vote brought Texas into the Union.
- In 1868, one vote saved President Andrew Jackson from being removed from office.
- In 1875, one vote changed France from a monarchy to a republic.
- In 1876, one vote gave Rutherford B. Hayes the presidency of the United States.
- In 1923, one vote gave Hitler leadership of the Nazi party.
- In 1942, one vote saved Selective Service (the military draft) just weeks before Pearl Harbor was attacked.[5]

What if one of those had been your vote?

Not to vote is irresponsible, and being irresponsible is one of the characteristics of a child. Your refusal to become identified with your country via the voting booth is childish. The government was given to you as a trust—you govern it by your vote. If you don't appreciate what your elected officials are doing, turn out the vote, and turn them out. Don't have a temper tantrum and not vote.

When black South Africans were finally given the right to vote, they stood in line for hours to cast their ballots. Denied for years, the vote became a sacred trust, and they meant to honor that above everything else.

Think. Act. Then feel the great relief and expansiveness of spirit when the results are in, the deed done, the success achieved.

Without doubt, however, our greatest responsibility is the trust of God's grace. I find it the most amazing thing known to man that God would trust us with His gospel—trust us to speak to that one person in need of salvation, without which no one shall see the Lord. What an absolutely awesome responsibility, and what an incredible privilege as well.

# CHAPTER SEVEN
## Life-Enhancement Christians

Godly leaders challenge the men of their day.

Gentlemen may cry peace, peace, but there is no peace. The war is actually begun!... Our brethren are already in the field.... What is it that gentlemen wish? What would they have? Is life so dear, or peace so sweet, as to be purchased at the price of chains and slavery? Forbid it Almighty God! I know not what course others may take, but as for me, give me liberty or give me death![1]

So said Patrick Henry to the Virginia Convention on May 23, 1775, and the following year on July 4, 1776, the Declaration of Independence was adopted.

When Joshua was leading the nation of Israel, he issued a similar challenge to the men of his day: "And if it seems evil to you to serve the LORD, choose for yourselves this day whom you will serve, whether the gods which your fathers served that were on the other side of the River, or the gods of the Amorites, in whose land you dwell. But as for me and my house, we will serve the LORD."[2]

Slogans disappear in time, but principles passed from generation to generation remain forever the same because they come from the Word of God. Every principle in human life emanates from, is initiated by, or originates in, the kingdom of God.

In the United States, the ideal of freedom is written and inscribed for every citizen to know, understand, and enjoy. Thomas Jefferson penned the final version of the Declaration of Independence after it was debated, altered, revised, and then accepted: "We hold these truths to be self-evident; that all men are created equal; that they are endowed by their creator with certain unalienable rights; that among these are life, liberty, and the pursuit of happiness."

I've heard it asked, "How can America be a secularist nation when it was founded under the stated belief that men are *created*, and that the *creator* gave them unalienable *rights*?" The answer can be seen in the history of Israel.

God brought Israel out of Egypt and bondage, through the Red Sea and wilderness. When they were ready to cross the Jordan, He wanted them to remember who did this for them. He instructed Joshua to erect a monument with twelve stones, to be a memorial to God's power to deliver. They were to tell it to their sons and pass the testimony to each new generation.

However, there "arose another generation . . . which knew not the LORD."[3] The fathers did not teach the truth to their sons, nor the sons to their sons. So the heritage of God's grace to the nation was lost. It can happen in any nation, including America.

Human liberty, personal freedom and dignity, family unity, and the ability to live, love, and work as one prospers are the "American Dream," and that of any people or nation. The basic dream of any man or country is to live in freedom.

Over the years, I have had the privilege of speaking to multilevel marketing groups, large and small. During these times, I'm with some great people. And, I've been in their Sunday services, when the people stay for another meeting where the gospel is presented. My first experience of this kind really affected me, when nearly five hundred people responded to the call of repentance and faith. It was marvelous!

One of the main tenets of such companies is the extolling of the "American Dream," or the "good life." Many times, though they predicate much of their success on principles, ethics, and personal integrity, they show the results of the dream in cars, boats, vacations, houses, and other economic benefits.

Some who attend see only the temporal and material benefits of Christianity. In many churches the same scenario has played out, with people answering the call to salvation only in hopes of achieving a better life on this earth. Someone coined a term for such people: "life-enhancement Christians."

## Life-Enhancement Christians

Though they may not look like it on the surface, life-enhancement Christians are still immature prodigals. They want the material benefits of Christianity—the promise of a better way of living, and the enjoyment of the self-improvement process—but they're unfamiliar with genuine repentance. Omitting repentance to get to faith, they engage in presumption. Presumption is not a substance. Faith is. Then, when their "faith," which is actually just presuming on God's grace, does not give them the desired results, they blame God.

Life-enhancement Christians share certain characteristics: They want a change of lifestyle, not a development in character. They act more like patched-up sinners than a new creation in Christ. They would enjoy the creature comforts of life, but miss the "call of God." They don't know the difference between an attack of Satan and conviction from the Holy Spirit. They lead spiritually insipid lives, with no taste for vital Christian experience.

They have a passion for God—strong feelings—but don't seem to understand that obedience is the evidence of love. Their rationalization of the word *love* allows them to "swing both ways," enjoying the world's way while attending church. But God says in His Word that such a lifestyle is actually spiritual adultery.[4]

Life-enhancement Christians also remind me of what's wrong with many evangelistic efforts today. Let me explain with a story.

In his book *Hell's Best Kept Secret*, Ray Comfort wrote about two men who were on an airplane. The flight attendants offered both of them parachutes to wear. The first man was told, "Please put this on. You will feel better, safer, and you'll enjoy the flight more."

The other attendant told the second man, "Put this on, because you'll need it when you jump. It's the only way you can be saved from death."

Both men put on their parachutes. Before long, though, the first man began to feel uncomfortable with the bulky pack; it was too restraining and didn't give him enough freedom to move. Eventually, he took it off. The second man, however, was determined to keep his parachute on no matter what, because he wanted more than anything else to be saved.[5]

In a similar way, too many people today are

encouraged to become Christians because it will help them and give them a better life, prosperity, and happiness. Their expectations are unrealistic. It makes the Cross of Christ of no effect.

The reality is that when we believe on Christ as our Savior, we will encounter persecution, tribulation, and rejection from the world.[6] When these come, life-enhancement Christians "take off" Christ.

True believers, mature Christians, realize there is "no other name under heaven . . . whereby we must be saved,"[7] and Jesus "delivers us from the wrath to come."[8] When true believers meet with tribulations and persecutions, they count it all joy for the knowledge of the hope that is set before them.[9] The difference between these two views is eternal in nature and consequence.

The men who died to give your nation freedom did not die because they wanted to enjoy the view from where you live. They died for freedom. In the same way, when we go to the Cross, we die to ourselves in order to live free in Christ.

"God forbid that I should boast except in the cross of our Lord Jesus Christ."[10]

# CHAPTER EIGHT

## Investing: Unconditionally, Sacrificially, Redemptively

The prodigal invested all he had in things that could not satisfy. That is still one of the saddest things to see: Men devote themselves to things, be they material—like cars or houses—or psychological—like prestige, position, power, or pride. Then like the prodigal, they watch them all disappear quickly, as vapor before the wind.

Even life-enhancement Christians put priorities on things personal rather than on those that are biblically spiritual, then they bow out when they're disappointed. "It works for others but not for me," they say as they leave God.

A teacher in a Christian school moved in with his girlfriend and they began to live together unmarried. When the administrator learned of it, he called in the teacher to question him about his change in living arrangements.

When the teacher admitted he was living with his girlfriend, the headmaster told him it was against school principles, it did not present a good role model for the students, and he would have to change or resign. The teacher resigned. But he complained loudly and bitterly, "We're Christians. We prayed about it and believe it's all right." Wrong!

Two young people were attending church, dating, and both seemed devoted to God. When they parted in their relationship, he went back to booze and drugs, and she became promiscuous and pregnant. Where was the Cross in their lives? What did Jesus really mean to them? Did they serve God only for what they could get—not what they could give Him? How much of themselves was invested in the kingdom of God?

Real satisfaction and fulfillment come from investing in relationships of genuine love and commitment—not from running from them in prodigal fashion, but rather from giving a relationship value by giving ourselves to it.

Our most important relationship, that deserving our greatest investment, is the one we have with God. But on the earthly plane, the most important relationship we have is with our spouses. And we invest in marriage to create the greatest possible value. Put another way, we are to love our wives as Christ loved the church.[1] He loves the church unconditionally, sacrificially, and redemptively.

Let me give you a simple analogy of redemptive love.

Pawnshops exist for people who need money but can't obtain it any other way. Let's take for example a man named Darrell, who entered one in such straits.

"I need a loan," he told the man behind the counter.

"What do you have for collateral?" answered the pawnbroker.

"Here's my watch," he said, showing the man his Rolex.

"I can loan you a couple of hundred."

"What?" Darrell exclaimed. "It's worth several thousand at least."

"Take it or leave it!"

After much negotiation, Darrell and the pawn-broker finally agreed on a loan amount. In exchange for the watch, the pawnbroker gave Darrell money and a redemption voucher. If Darrell came back within ninety days and repaid the broker what he had borrowed, with interest, he would get his watch back. If he didn't redeem the watch, the broker had the right to dispose of it as he saw fit. After all, he was in business to make money.

The transaction was based on Darrell giving his word and the broker wanting collateral to confirm it. Now only time would tell if Darrell would get the watch back. His watch was in the custody of the pawnbroker. The only way to have it returned was to redeem it according to the agreed-upon terms. His watch was only as safe as his word was good.

God watches over His Word to perform, or fulfill, it. The prophet, Jeremiah, heard God say: "Thou hast well seen: for I will hasten my word to perform it."[2] Jesus Christ is our Redeemer, through His redemptive work on Calvary, and proves it every day by performing, or fulfilling, His Word to us.

Because we are created in the image of God, whatever God's Word is to Him, our word is to be to us. We, too, are to watch over our word to perform it.

Darrell had to take care to perform his word, or he would lose his watch. The watch belongs to Darrell, but it is in the custody of the pawnbroker until he redeems it. By redeeming it, he keeps his word—and his watch.

As with Darrell, his watch, and the pawnbroker, so it is with a man and his wife. When a man gives his wife his word, he must watch over it to perform it. That's one major way he shows his love to her and loves her redemptively. He redeems, or keeps, his word by hastening to perform or fulfill it.

The performance of the promise is the measure of a man. A man's character is shown more clearly by how he keeps his word than any other way. It's called integrity.

When a man gives his wife his word and doesn't perform it, she retains custody of it, even though it is his word. She retains custody of every unfulfilled promise, every word not performed. She may eventually dispose of it as she will. When she gets so much of it, she may decide she doesn't want any more of it—or of him—and dispose of them as she will.

Investing yourself in your marriage also means the use of money. In one of our men's events, a man walked up to me at break time, got right in my face, and said, "You cost me $55,000!"

I was startled to say the least, and I started to stammer something when he continued.

"Sitting in the front row of church one night, I heard you make the statement that a married woman's basic security is in the man she marries, more than in her home," he stated. "You pointed your finger and looked right at me and said 'He is to give his wife security.' Identity, stability, and security, you said, were God's provisions to us, and ours to our family. But, you said, if he has a 'renter's mentality,' she doesn't have the same security as if she owns her own home. I was agreeing with you until you said that.

"I went home and asked my wife if she wanted to own a home. She said she had always wanted one. I told her my parents had always rented, and so that's what I did. I didn't know she wanted the security of her own home. It was a revelation to me.

"We went right out and bought a home, and that's how much it cost," he concluded. Then he laughed.

"Has it made your relationship better?" I asked.

"Ten thousand percent, and I thank you for it!"

I related that story in another meeting, and months afterward another gentleman told me my message cost him $28,000 for a home. Some men in today's major cities would think these men got off pretty cheap! But it made a difference in the marriage.

God's love is manifested in the Cross of Christ. Jesus came to us in His righteousness and became identified with our sin, that we might come to Him in our sin and become identified with His righteousness. It's an eternal exchange. God loves redemptively. We can only love as He does if His Spirit is in us producing such redeeming grace.

The evidences of Christ's love are selflessness, a desire for the benefit of the one loved, and a desire for unity. A man is to love his wife in that same way. And he invests in her unconditionally, sacrificially, and redemptively.

# CHAPTER NINE

## Owe No Man

As the old saying goes, you'll never see a hearse pulling a U-Haul trailer. The only things we can take with us when we die are our relationships—with God and other people. Relationships have eternal value. What's true in eternity is also true in the here and now.

It's true, too, that anything of value comes only at a cost. The more precious something is, the greater the value it has for us, the higher the cost. This is true not only with cars, houses, and antiques, but it is true in relationships such as in marriage.

But the most precious relationship, which comes

at the highest cost, is our relationship with our Creator! His Word is the sole source of our faith and the absolute rule of our conduct. Obedience to His Word can cost us everything. No matter what it may cost us, it is nothing in comparison to the price He paid for us on Calvary.

Although things that are invisible are the most intrinsically valuable, it is the things that are visible for which we pay the most money. Money establishes values in our lives. What we expend on our wives shows her worth to us. And what we invest in our children reveals their importance to us. But what we expend and invest involves far more than just money.

What are we willing to invest to establish—and maintain—friendships?

Frank and Sharon were friends of mine who had worked with me for years. We had worked side by side through all the blessings and vicissitudes of our lives together. But finally the day came for them to leave to pursue their own dreams, and I handled it poorly.

In their leaving, I managed to offend them both. They did pursue their dream and watched it come to fruition. But I carried with me the burden of a lost relationship for almost two years. During that time there did not seem to be a place or a time that our friendship could be repaired, reconciled, and restored.

Then one day when I went to a mutual friend's house to watch football, Frank and Sharon were there. We acknowledged one another briefly and stayed in different rooms. But eventually I was able to approach Frank privately and say, "Step into the next room with me, will you?"

Standing in front of him, I reached up and put my arms around his neck and looked him straight in the eye.

"I want to repent to you. God doesn't want our apologies, but our repentance. Neither do you need my apology, but my repentance. I repent.

"What I did to you and your wife offended you. It hurt you both. I'm genuinely sorry for what I did. All I can do is repent to you and ask you to forgive me.

"It was probably time for you to leave, but the manner of leaving was not pleasing to God, you, your wife, the ministry, or me. So, as much as there is in me, by the help of God, I want to repent and ask you to forgive me.

"I only want to remember the good things you did—the good that you contributed to me and the ministry. I do not want you, or me, either, to ever remember anything but the good things we shared together in our lives. Forgive me."

He looked at me keenly, paused, then said he forgave me.

"You say it in word," I told him. "But, you haven't said it in spirit or gesture. You will need to pray, ask God to help you, and when the day comes that you can really do it, let's get together again."

We left the room, and I went to his wife, who was sitting on a couch. I sat down next to her and whispered in her ear the same words I had said aloud to Frank. I saw a tear form and run down her cheek before she wiped it away.

She turned to me and said, "Thanks, I needed that."

Weeks later Frank came to me, and we sat and talked and let God heal the relationship. I saw Sharon with my wife a few weeks later, and it was as though nothing had ever gone wrong.

The reason I went to them was because I owed it to them. "Keep out of debt and owe no man anything, except to love one another," is what the Bible says.[1] To keep out of debt and obey God's Word, I needed to pay them what I owed them—my repentance. Today, I am out of debt—I owe them nothing except to love them. I am "debt-free."

"Live debt-free" is more than a slogan, it is a way of life that God wants for us. To make that happen, He gave Christ to pay the debt, so we could live free from sin.

I mentioned this one day to a friend named Greg.

"Ed, I see it!" he almost shouted. "My son and I went to a counselor. She was talking to my son when he blurted out, 'My dad promised to take me camping, twice he promised to take me fishing. My dad owes me!'

"It's clear why the Bible says the debtor is the servant to the lender.[2] Only for me it means that I am a debtor to my son, and the reason he won't listen to me is because he feels like I owe him. He'll never listen to me until I pay my debt to him."

We sat together for a few more minutes, and I explained to him about giving his word to his son. Because the father had not performed his word, his son had custody of it. Until he performed or fulfilled his word to his son, he had not kept it—he needed to pay the price to redeem his word.

His was a prodigal problem. We are all prodigals in our actions apart from God. When we act without the influence or control of the Holy Spirit in our lives, prodigal problems occur.

The price the prodigal paid to be reconciled and restored to his father was to admit he was wrong, humble himself to ask forgiveness, and throw himself on the father's mercy. That is a pattern for us all. It's the way of the Cross—but more on that later.

The other day I called my friend and asked how things were going with his son. He told me, "I am planning a camping trip for the family. We're going to do a little fishing and just take some time together."

The price of relationships is not measured in dollars, but in the willingness to pay what is owed at the cost of self. Debt is one of the devil's methods to stifle relationships. Keep out of debt.

Relationships are the treasure of heaven. There are none in hell. As someone said, "Life is hell without a friend." Pay whatever price is necessary to make sure your relationships are found in God—both here and in heaven.

# CHAPTER TEN

## Covenant, Not Contract

The members of the wedding party were hurrying and scurrying to ready themselves, putting everything in proper order. Last-minute details were passed from the bridegroom to his father concerning what needed to be done immediately after the ceremony.

Then, just fifteen minutes before the bridegroom and the attendants were to take their places, one of them offered some good counsel. He, himself, had just been married a month before.

"Man," he told the bridegroom, "this wedding night isn't only for your pleasure. It's also for hers, and don't you forget it. How you treat her tonight will determine how she reacts to you in future nights. You need to be tender, thoughtful, caring, and loving, letting her know by your actions how much you love her.

"Unlike other guys, you haven't slept with anyone before, and she hasn't been with anyone either. You have kept your virginity, and we all admire you for that. But tonight has got to be good. If you're abrupt with her sexually or in the way you talk to her or if you only want to satisfy yourself at her expense, you're going to pay for it. Maybe for most of your marriage. If you cause her to dislike the sexual relationship, it will affect you in more ways than you want to know about."

Men suffer from wavering with such commitments. A double-minded man is unstable in all his ways, and a thoughtless person will suffer in every area of his life, especially if he's thoughtless with his wife. He creates his own prodigal problems with her, then looks to her to provide the solution.

Marriage is a covenant, not a contract. That's a crucial distinction. In the wedding vows that are used so often, the aspect of covenant in a marriage is made apparent. But it is good to be reminded that there is a difference between a covenant and a contract.

Contracts are used to make agreements between people. Contracts are only as good as the character of those who sign them. They're for specific matters and are limited to what's in the agreement. Signing a prenuptial agreement (contract) is based on the fact that the parties involved question each other's motives or they don't believe they'll live together for the rest of their lives. It denotes a lack of trust. Trust is basic to a covenant, including marriage.

A marriage covenant is when two people love and trust each other with their entire lives and are totally vulnerable and committed to care for each other to the death. God is a covenant-making God, and it was He who established marriage as a covenant relationship.

Unlike contracts, there are no limits to liability in a covenant. Treating marriage vows as simply a contractual agreement between two parties demeans covenant. Lawyers make their livings writing contracts. Contracts can be annulled, rendered void, or just torn up. What may benefit the legal profession does not necessarily honor God.

When a husband and wife make their commitment to each other a covenant instead of a contract, their relationship usually gets better and better over the years. And one of the most enjoyable ways they can honor each other is to renew their vows.

My friend Gavin MacLeod once recommended me to the Princess Cruise Lines to join a "Love Boat" cruise and perform the renewal of the vows for the couples on board. Nancy and I loved the cruise and the great time we had with Gavin and his wife, Patti.

More than six hundred couples gathered on the top deck on Valentine's Day at 8:00 A.M. for the ceremony.

As the men and women faced each other and recited their marriage vows, some actually had tears in their eyes from the reality of the sacrament and the affection it generated. It was at once so solemn, yet tender and filled with meaning, that everyone was uplifted. People talked about it throughout the rest of the cruise.

Two days after the ceremony, a Philadelphia television station broadcast its morning talk show live by satellite from the ship. Four couples from the Philadelphia area who had taken part were there to tell what the ceremony had meant to them. As the host of the program interviewed them, their statements of what they had experienced affected me deeply.

They told the television audience what their original marriage ceremonies had been like. Some of them indicated that they were so nervous, tense, or strained at their weddings that they didn't even remember what was said. One person hadn't appreciated the minister. And, if I remember correctly, one of them had celebrated too much the night before the wedding and didn't remember it at all!

All of them said, however, that the renewal of vows meant more to them than the original ceremony. They now had several years of experience in marriage, could appreciate what the words meant, and could say them with devotion and love, valuing their partner now more than before. So many others told me the same things during the days following that I determined that I would encourage everyone who has been married for any length of time to renew their vows. Such a ceremony gives new momentum to the relationship, a fresh start in some ways, and a revitalized commitment to each other and the marriage.

Real love is not all warmth and excitement, enthusiasm and desire, but is about the welfare of the other—looking after each other's interests, fighting *for* (not just with) one another, and caring for the marriage partner even more than for self. The renewal of vows gives a forum to accomplish and confess that in truth. This kind of renewal is an understanding of what has been, a resolution to forgive the errors of the past, a look forward to the future with a heart of gratitude for the faithfulness of the one loved, and an expression of faith in God to regenerate the union.

Forgiveness is essential to longevity in marriage. And forgiveness is a manifestation of grace, making it real. Where there is little grace in marriage, unforgiveness will shut it down.

Grace is defined as unmerited or undeserved favor that comes from love. Today there is so little grace apparent in human life that you wonder how any marriage stays together. I've jokingly said, with a touch of realism, that the reason my wife is the epitome of Christian grace is that I've given her a lifetime of praying to forgive me. But, it's true that without God's grace, we wouldn't still be married.

## Covenant, Not Contract

In the great majority of cases, there's no excuse for divorce. Jesus gave only two reasons for it, and then said they were given only because of people's hardness of heart.[1] That's still true. The common thinking about divorce is that the one filing for it is the person who is hard of heart. To me, that is not so. Having counseled women, talked to their husbands, and prayed about their difficult relationships over the years, I have come to the conclusion that too many times the hardness of heart is contained in the unwillingness to listen, change, or to even consider the consequences of what is happening, whomever it may be.

I once counseled a lady who was filing for divorce. It was against everything she had ever been taught, something she did not believe was right, but it seemed to be her only "escape." Her husband would not listen to her, absolutely would not consider going to a counselor, and failed to even consider meeting her needs even though she had spent twenty-one years meeting his.

She went back to school, graduated with honors, joined a company, was promoted, brought her pay-check to him, and was getting nothing out of the marriage. Even the sex was mechanical and stale. She grew to a new level of life, developed friendships, even changed the way she looked and dressed, and still he remained the same. He made no attempt to be a part of what she was doing but demanded that she do what he pleased. A selfish heart is the hardest heart.

"Marriage is honorable in all," so be an honorable man.[2]

If the passion has faded in your relationship—if you've fallen into a rut—if you and your wife disagree more than you agree—if you fight more than you make up—if you are not still on the same level with each other, and don't care—if your heart and eye begin to wander—your marriage isn't in trouble. It's dying! Don't waste years of your life—ask God to resurrect your marriage!

Hard hearts generally break after divorce. If you could read the heartbroken letters I get from men who say to me, "Ed, if I had it to do all over again, I'd do it differently." Don't do it all over again, just start doing it differently now. Renew your vows before God. Mean them. And pray for His resurrection power.

# CHAPTER ELEVEN

## Mercy Triumphs over Judgment

We don't have to find ourselves in a pigsty to recognize our need for mercy. As prodigals, we all make mistakes at times and need mercy.

When I first met Bruce and learned of his way of life, I appreciated him greatly, and over the years I added a measure of admiration to that esteem. But Bruce's dream almost became a nightmare.

Bruce's dream was to have a wife, a family, and a career—and he was living it. He had two lovely daughters and a job with a major airline. Life was good.

Then, his wife told him she was leaving him and

the girls. Suddenly Bruce was faced with some choices he hadn't anticipated. When his divorce was finalized, he chose to forgo his career in favor of his two daughters. For years, he maintained his family with a part-time job with the airline, passing up many opportunities for promotion and better pay. It meant having to do without and living a scaled-down version of the California "good life."

He lived in an older home and drove an older—much older—car, but he was home every day when his daughters returned from school. He considered being there for them more important than the material benefits others enjoyed. Their consolation was that, with the airline job, he could take his daughters places others might not get to go.

Bruce learned to be chef, housekeeper, and nurturer of his daughters. His domestic skills only enhanced his manliness. He was a good father, and I admired his resolve, dedication, and love for his children.

The thought of remarriage was foreign to him for years. He didn't lack opportunity for female companionship, but mostly he denied it as neither promiscuity nor marriage could encroach on his loyalty to his God and his daughters. He didn't lack desire to love and marry again, but the breakup of his marriage was so devastating that he hesitated to risk love again. He continued in his own steadfast way just living, laughing, and, somewhere in the back of his mind, waiting for the right woman to come along.

At work, Bruce began to converse more and more often with another employee, Jill, and finally he began dating her. She seemed the perfect fit for his description of the kind of woman he would love to marry. But when I mentioned this to him, he just laughed and gave me the old line, "We're just friends."

"Friends" meant she eventually fixed dinner at his house, counseled his daughters, shared in his family's recreational times, and spent more and more time with him. This went on for three years, with me and others wanting to know if it was serious. When asked, however, Bruce said it would be nice, but "not yet."

Finally one day Jill told him, "This is going nowhere, so let's just quit it now!" She broke off the relationship, and he was devastated. His "not yet" became her "no way."

Three days of loneliness and longing made Bruce realize he didn't want to live without her. It dawned on him that if he really felt that way, he must really love her. So he set about trying to win her back.

But, try as he might, Jill would not go beyond greetings at work, turning down any suggestion of dating. After a week of this, Bruce drove to her house one evening, found another car parked in front, and after returning home, he spent the night wondering what was going on. Thinking about some other man courting her was mental and emotional torture.

In desperation, he called his good friend Jack.

"What am I going to do?" he almost cried into the phone. "I've lost her due to my own stupidity. Why didn't I recognize how much she meant to me and how much I loved her before she was gone? Now she wants nothing to do with me."

A long discussion ensued, then Jack gave Bruce some wisdom.

"Bruce," he said, "there's a verse in the Bible that says, 'Mercy triumphs over judgment.'[1] When mercy comes in, judgment has to leave. You've been living under the judgment of your decision. Now you need the mercy of God. Ask Him for mercy. Ask

Him for another opportunity with her. Trust God's mercy."

That wasn't just good advice. It was godly counsel. It was a word that had life. It was quick, powerful, and sharper than any two-edged sword.[2] Penetrating Bruce's mind and heart, it became the foundation for his prayer.

Mercy! He would pace the floor at night, crying that word, asking God to give him favor once again in Jill's eyes.

After several days and nights, Bruce took courage and asked Jill to go to dinner with him just one more time. She agreed. He was elated. Thanking God continually, he made plans for the evening.

She wouldn't let him pick her up; she said she would meet him at the restaurant. He chose her favorite spot. Arriving three hours early, Bruce arranged with the maître d' the table he wanted. Bruce told him, the chef, and all the waiters what this dinner meant. He gave some roses to the waiters and asked them to bring one to Jill every ten minutes that night.

When she arrived and was seated, they ordered dinner for the evening. Immediately, Bruce began to talk, and he didn't stop for three hours. He told Jill how he knew he had failed her, how much he missed her, how deeply and truly he loved her, that without her life wasn't worth living, and that he would be the man he promised to be when they had first started dating. Meanwhile, every ten minutes, a waiter arrived with another rose.

Jill barely touched her dinner, Bruce's turned cold, and the waiters' supply of roses ran out. When Bruce finally believed it was time, he slid off his chair, knelt by hers, took her hand, and said, "Jill, will you marry me?"

She looked into his eyes and saw his genuine love. "Yes, Bruce," she said. "That's all I ever wanted."

"Yes!" he exclaimed. "She said *yes*!" He jumped to his feet and ran around the restaurant, telling everyone she had said yes. The waiters clapped, the maître d' brought the dessert, people smiled, and Jill just laughed at her new fiancé. Mercy had triumphed over judgment.

If, as you read this, you're suffering from judgment brought on by a wrong decision you've made or the failure to make a decision, there's mercy for you. God is merciful and His love is manifested in grace, the essence of grace being mercy, and the greatest act of mercy being forgiveness. He's not willing that any should perish—not in sin, from mistakes, or from bad decisions. He is able to apply mercy where judgment is, and turn your life around. You, too, can experience mercy. It's there right now for you because of God's Word: "Mercy triumphs over judgment."[3]

At the Los Angeles Coliseum, after I spoke to the more than 72,000 Promise Keepers there, I was walking back up the steps when someone handed me a card that said, "This man says you know him, and he wants to speak to you."

When I went outside the gate and saw who it was, we greeted each other, and he reached around me in a big bear hug, then whispered in my ear, "Forgive me, and ask Lois to forgive me. I'm sorry. When you said that about God watching over His Word to perform it, it just pierced my heart, and I had to see you."

I hadn't seen the man in seventeen years. Back then, he had been engaged to marry my daughter, Lois. My wife and Lois had arranged the church, parson, flowers, and photographer, and in two months, the marriage was to take place.

When I walked through my door one evening, however, my wife's eyes were red from crying, and my daughter was lying on the couch with the blanket pulled over her face. The atmosphere was ghastly.

"What happened?" I asked my wife softly.

"He just called wanting to postpone the wedding," she answered. I knew who "he" was. It must not have been more than thirty seconds at the most, but it seemed like hours as the two of us stood there, with me taking in the situation.

"We're not going to postpone the wedding. We're going to cancel it," I said. "If he doesn't have enough manhood to keep his word, he doesn't have enough character to marry my daughter."

Nancy and Lois undid all they could, and Lois thanked me many times over the years for that decision. I never gave it or him another thought. We went about our business, and it was done. I've written about it before and used it as a classic example of a man who couldn't keep his word.

Now, seventeen years later, I was facing the man, with him asking my forgiveness. "Of course I forgive you," I told him. "Be free in the name of the Lord." In that moment, we both became "debt-free."

Later, as I recounted the experience to my wife, she asked, "Did you ever think of what he must have been living under these last seventeen years? The judgment he was living under? And he was never able to be free from it until you forgave him. It must have been awful! How many fathers would cancel a wedding the way you did? How many men would make that kind of decision?"

She made her point, both from my standpoint and from his.

For seventeen years, he lived under the judgment of my decision, and he was never free from it until mercy triumphed in the forgiveness he was given.

God's Word says mercy triumphs over judgment, that when mercy comes in, judgment has to go. Mercy will triumph in your life also—right now! You no longer need to live under the judgment of your actions, or sins, or those of others. God's mercy is available this very moment. Begin to ask, because you have not if you ask not.[4] This could be your answer right now for your need. Receive it in

Christ's name. Don't live under judgment another minute.

"Through the LORD's mercies we are not consumed."[5] Not consumed by judgment, fear, failure, guilt, or condemnation, but set free through the mercy of God.

# CHAPTER TWELVE

## The Eternity Hidden in Time and Money

Our Christian Men's Network has been operating in Great Britain for years, and for some time it was organized and promoted by Eric Hutchinson. A rugby player turned church pastor, he was a man's man.

When Eric was diagnosed with cancer, he confronted his doctor about the prognosis for his disease. He had to press the doctor because the doctor was reluctant to give Eric any bad news.

"Tell me, Doctor," Eric asked, "what do you think? How long do I have, if God doesn't heal me?"

"Well, I can't promise you more than six months," the doctor said slowly.

"Well, that's great," Eric quickly responded, "because I can't promise you tomorrow!"

None of us have a guarantee of life beyond this present breath. Eric used his comment as a springboard to ask the doctor about his eternal destiny. Ever eager to see others know Christ, not even a "death sentence" could diminish Eric's desire to take as many people as he could reach to the Father's house with him.

Eric was right. We have no second chance to live today. Today, this moment, is all we have, and we get to live it just one time. Eternity seems far away, yet it's with us at this moment. That's why it is vital that we make the most of every day and every opportunity that comes our way.

God says a lot about time management. For instance, "To everything there is a season, / A time for every purpose under heaven."[1]

In the book *Strong Men in Tough Times*, I wrote, "The man without an organized system of thought will always be at the mercy of the man who has one."[2]

To organize is to show respect for something. Respect is an intangible that has tangible results. God in His Word tells the man to love his wife, and the wife to respect her husband.[3] The reason for this is that you cannot submit to what you don't respect. Loss of respect is the number one cause of divorce. That's true in a marriage, and also true between pastor and parishioner.

Organization shows respect for time. Men who fail to organize their personal, family, or professional lives actually show disrespect for their own lives and the contributions of those with whom they have relationship. They live under self-induced stress and are always at the mercy of those who respect time.

Procrastination, like disorganization, shows disrespect for time, self, and others. It produces pressure on self and stress on others. It steals time, kills initiative, and destroys production.

Healthy spontaneity, on the other hand, is always based on good preparation, whether it be in a business decision, a family outing, sermon, or the intimate relationship between a husband and wife. But procrastination doesn't allow for good preparation and is therefore an impairment to spontaneity.

Time, like fruit, ripens. Fruit spoils if it is picked too late, and it's sour if it is picked too soon. Likewise, success comes from being the right man at the right time in the right place. Taking time to listen to your family shows respect for them, and any time is always the right time to do that. But giving time to foolish people shows disrespect for self.

We must winnow time, as we do words, to remove the chaff and leave the wheat—to dismiss the invalid and retain the valid. Not every word spoken to us deserves to be retained. Not every demand is worthy of our time. Often we allow others to impose on us and sap our time and energy. We must discipline ourselves to respect our own time.

Organization of time also allows for good relationships. It begets peace, whereas disorganization brings conflict and disharmony. Harmony comes from the accord of strains of music blended together to form melodious sounds. Symphonies are composed of notes organized in "arrangements," all making harmony together.

God calls for the same in His church. Psalm 133:1–3 (TLB) says, "How wonderful it is, how pleasant, when brothers live in harmony! For harmony is as precious as the fragrant anointing oil.... [It] is as refreshing as the dew on Mount Hermon, on the mountains of Israel." Harmony in the home is a sweet sound. Harmony in the church is a melodious symphony. Proper use of time is vital for both.

I'll never forget the words spoken by my friend A. R. Bernard at a 1996 Summit meeting: "We stifle creativity by spending too much time on maintenance." We make progress by using our creativity while maintaining service. Determining when and how each is provided is wisdom. Men who only "maintain" a marriage rather than using creativity to increase its value and pleasure misuse their time and talent. Ministers who major in "maintaining" their congregation instead of moving to do greater things become a "lid" rather than a "covering" for their people.

All of us in the Christian Men's Network, are not simply trying to maintain what we have, but to respect the precious time we have left to reach a world in need, "submitting to one another in the fear of God."[4]

One of the major ways God made every man equal is by giving each of us exactly twenty-four hours a day. God gives the same amount to drug addicts, executives, and preachers. How we use it shows our level of respect for God's gift.

The time we once had, we no longer have. It is gone forever, never to return. Time is eternal in its immensity and character. Yet it has form and function only when it becomes the present. The time we are to have is yet to come. Time comes to us from out of the future and has no limit except when it comes to us.

Time is filled with opportunities, possibilities, promises, great and good gifts, and mercies that are new and fresh every day.

As time leaves us and goes into the past, it becomes yesterday, last week, last month, last year, and continues on into the distant past and is called history. History is the experience of the past to teach us what we need today to provide for the future.

All we retain from the past is based on what we did when it was today. That's why what we do today has the possibility of both good and bad, both in the present and for eternity.

The Bible is unique because it holds the eternity of the *future* in its *present* writings taken from the *past*. When we act on God's Word today, the promise of the future given in the past becomes real in the present.

Money is like time in many respects. They're both but a means to an end, not an end in themselves. When money becomes an end, it becomes a matter of lust, not love, and greed is its character. Lust is insatiable. When lusted after, money can never satisfy. Only when money is a means to an end, based on charity, can it ever truly satisfy. Like time, it must be converted to good, not perverted to evil.

We're able to do things with money today that will last for eternity. We work to get money in order to do good for ourselves and others. But it often takes a combination of time and money to do the good that will last forever.

Nancy and I bought used bedroom furniture and used it for years and years. Finally, when some extra money came our way, we bought new furniture. About the same time, we received a letter from a ministry that stated its critical need at the moment, and we sent a liberal offering. Time and money combined allowed us to do something good for ourselves and the kingdom of God. With the expenditure for the furniture, *we* were blessed. With the offering, we blessed God.

The money we spent on furniture had tomorrow in it. The money we gave away had eternity in it. It took the combination of time and money to make them both possible.

My good friend Dr. Dino Delaportas called me from Hagerstown, Maryland, to tell me something.

Ed, before you were here last time for an event, the youth pastor of my church called and wanted me to agree with him in prayer that his father would attend. I was happy to do it.

The day of the event, he waited in the lobby for his dad, but he never showed until after the meeting had started. Then he had to sit right down in the front . . . all the back rows were filled.

When you called for men to make their decision for Christ, confess Him publicly, the dad went forward. He really got saved.

In the second session, you stopped speaking, looked at him, and asked if he would do what you asked. He was hesitant but agreed. You gave him one hundred dollars and told him to take his wife to dinner after church the next day and tell her what God had done in his life.

The problem was, he had divorced his wife years earlier. But after a couple of weeks, he called his ex-wife on the phone, told her what happened, and wondered if he could fly down to the state where she lived and take her to dinner. She agreed.

Yesterday the youth pastor called me again. He said his mother called to tell him that for the last year, since that meeting, she and his father had been dating long-distance and now they were going to remarry.

She wanted to know if the youth pastor would marry them.

We both laughed on the phone. The youth pastor's money when he bought his dad a ticket to the event had eternity in it. The use of money has eternity in it.

Martin Fessler is a missionary to Mexico from San Antonio, Texas. His brother, Dick, wanted to help him in his ministry, so he paid for the Spanish translation of our *Communication, Sex, and Money* video series. That was ten years ago. The other day we received a call in our offices from someone telling us that they were showing that series in Argentina. It's still changing lives. Dick's offering to the ministry had eternity in it. "Lay up for yourselves treasures in heaven," Jesus said.[5]

The prodigal wasted both the time and money that represented his life. But when he "came to his senses," he had both in abundance in the Father's house.

When Byron became a Christian at one of our men's meetings, he was living like a prodigal. He was a party animal spending his time and money on drugs and drinking. After his conversion, when he returned to his Father's house, someone told him about tithing. He inquired as to what it meant, and he was told that the tithe belongs to the Lord.

"What's a tithe?" he wanted to know.

"It is the first ten percent of all you make," they answered.

"Is that all? The devil's been getting about ninety percent of what I make. That's nothing. No problem!"

When the prodigal comes home, everything changes.

Think of what you spent on a wasted life, and can God have less? Think of what the lawyers make if you divorce, and can you spare your wife less? Everything you spent time and money on in prodigal living went to hell. Now that you're back to the Father's house, it has eternity in it and is to be used to the glory of God. Nothing is too good for our heavenly Father. He gave His best for us. Let's give Him our best.

# CHAPTER THIRTEEN

## Cleaning the Closet

I was doing some repair work in a house when I was newly married and seeking some additional income. I vividly remember walking by a table with a big, juicy apple. I still remember it because it marked me. I was tempted to eat it, but I did not have the home-owner's permission. Therein was the test of character. I could have done it. The homeowner may not have even cared. But still I didn't do it. No matter how slight or powerful the temptation (it could have been a Rolex watch on that table), the test of character is always based on the ability to resist temptation.

I talked recently with some men whom I had previously known, and it was as though I had never known them, though I thought I had in years gone by. What had been was not, and what I hoped was not, was.

One of them, whom I'll call Albert, told me that his life had been a charade—that he was just a good actor and his whole life had been one long lie. He said he was tired of pretending, lying, trying to present himself as something he was not. Albert told me he was a homosexual, and that he was sick of trying to live "straight."

"No more," he told me. "I'm tired of living a lie. So, I'm going to stop being hypocritical and be me."

It was hard to listen to him. I had admired Albert for his talent, respected him for his commitment to truth, and lauded him as one of my heroes. Hearing him tell me of this left me emotionally drained, socially deserted, and spiritually devastated.

"Rather than hold to the marriage and occasionally slip out to meet a man and try to hide it from my teammates," Albert continued, "I'm leaving all of it to find a man."

Ouch!

## Cleaning the Closet

"I want to be a man of integrity, so I'm not going to live like I have any longer. Sporadically slipping out to be with a man while pretending to be something I'm not is not right. I'm tired of being a bisexual."

I flashed back to a night at Constitution Hall in Washington, D.C., at one of our events. During a break as I was walking away for a moment of rest, a man approached me and grabbed my arm. "I know you are busy, but I want to tell you that what you are doing is right on."

At the close of the morning session, I had asked for those who wanted to be free of the homosexual lifestyle to come forward for prayer.

"I was bisexual for twenty-four years," he told me as we walked. "I thought no one knew, but after Jesus delivered me I found out everyone knew.

"My wife has forgiven me, my two sons have forgiven me; and, being straight now—not having the guilt and confusion—my life is the best ever."

I could not help but remember his words as I sat talking to Albert. I looked at the man seated across from me in the coffee shop and asked, "If you think you can be a practicing homosexual and still be a

Christian, then why can't I as a heterosexual live in adultery and still be an upstanding and acceptable Christian? Aren't they both sex sins?"

"What about the men who divorce their wives without the cause Christ talks about in the Bible?" he said in answer. "Aren't they living in adultery?"

"Tell me something," I finally said. "Are you satisfied with homosexuality?"

"Of course," Albert said. "It's not the sexual thing, though. It's just having a man's arms around you that is so good." As he said it, we both knew he was lying. He was saying something totally incongruous to me. But, my conversation with him made me bold enough to continue asking questions.

"Do you really find men attractive?" I asked.

"Yes, in the same way you find women attractive."

"Yes, but I don't look on women as objects of self-gratification," I said. "That's also sex sin. What about family, friends, men you've been on teams with? What kind of role model are you going to present to young people—even your own children?" I asked.

"That's not my problem. I don't want a divorce, but I don't want to live with her either. What they want to say about it is up to them."

## Cleaning the Closet

Albert wanted everything both ways, so that he wouldn't have to give up anything and whatever was done would always be someone else's fault. Ultimate self-justification.

He was going to put everyone through such hurtful humiliation, particularly and specifically his family, cause them to face shame and sorrow, yet he didn't want to talk about them. It seemed so callow to me. Albert was talking about being so courageous one minute, yet he was displaying such a juvenile cowardice the next. He talked about maintaining his integrity, then lied to me.

Albert reminded me of the historical truth about Abraham and Lot. When Abraham gave Lot, his nephew, the choice of where he wanted to live, Canaan or the valley between, Lot chose the valley. The Bible says he pitched his tents *toward* Sodom and Gomorrah, but when Abraham rescued him from the destruction of those two cities, he found Lot living *in* them.[1]

"Are you going to marry some man?" I wanted to know.

"I don't plan on it."

"What about the people we see who are so vicious

and violent in their behavior—raiding churches, throwing feces on the altar, threatening churchgoers, throwing condoms as water balloons at the congregation?"

"Those are activists. I'm not into that either. Those of us in our Bible study group just want to live our lives as homosexuals and be accepted as normal people. We're not into that perverted kind of stuff."

Now, I was really astounded. But more than that, a great sorrow at such a gross deception welled up in me. It hurt.

I had had a similar conversation with another man who had once been my hero, and told him how I admired him for overcoming his temptation, but he also went back to the homosexual lifestyle.

When we met before he cut off his Christian friends, I pressed him. "What if I were to have an affair with your wife while you were having an affair with another man? What would you say to that?"

"You'd be wrong," he answered.

What?!

God is not the author of confusion, and these are *very* confused men. They want their sexual impurity and to still be able to keep their relationship with God. Yet if I wanted the same, hetereosexually, I'd be sinning.

Yet, in the book of Acts, one of the stringent applications of lifestyle was put upon Gentile believers to "refrain from sexual impurity.[2] It's there. It can't be denied.

The "hardness of heart" in these men is causing them to divorce themselves from everything and everyone they have known in the past and to give themselves over to a lifestyle they formerly said they hated. I wondered, *Do they still hate it but lie to themselves and others because the deception and temptation are so great?*

They were divorcing themselves not just from their wives, but also from a lifetime of friendships and the social structure they had always lived within. It seemed they were turning their back on everything near and dear.

Above all, they were putting Christ to an open shame.

One of them told me that years before when he had faced this issue and seemingly conquered it, he had lied about it. "I just told you what you wanted to hear," he said. "I didn't believe it, but it satisfied you, and it was what you wanted."

I have met enough former homosexuals to know the torment their choices bring. To me it seemed the truth wasn't in him. He had once told the truth, but now covered it up to justify his decision not to live by truth.

For years I have stated the axiomatic principle that all adulterers, alcoholics, abusers, and addicts are liars. It's their form of denial to justify their deception.

I remember when I left my friend at the coffee shop. Until he disappeared into the distance, I stood hoping he'd return—to me, to Christ, to his wife. Instead, he walked into his darkness, and I left to return to the life, light, and love of my wife.

I went home to my dream, and he left to enter his nightmare.

The sympathy and compassion I felt for them was sometimes mixed with anger. I had been betrayed. I had been lied to. Worse, the Cross had been betrayed. Man in his arrogance had lied even to God.

I scheduled an appointment with the wife of one of the men and told her how I'd tried to counsel her husband. With tears and a pained face, she said she still prayed he would come to his right mind, that God would work a miracle in his mind and heart and restore him to a right relationship with Himself and his family. Hoping the prodigal would come home, she was the epitome of the axiom "Hope springs eternal."

She told me she would take him back in an instant if he would give up his homosexuality. When I questioned her certainty, she said, "Even in light of all he has done, I would take him back. I love him. Our children love him."

She was pleading with and for him, not with me, even though she was talking to me. She wasn't even thinking of herself, only of the man she had loved and lived with for so many years. Sounds like the heart of the "Father" and His great love were in her heart. Yet her yesterday's joys were being swallowed up by today's sorrows.

Thinking of them, her, and what has happened, a great sense of loss grips me, and with it, a deep anger toward the deceiver of men. My thoughts were of the first Adam in the garden and how he rationalized his behavior to justify his transgression of God's command. Rationalization is the form of deception that allows men to justify their unconscionable acts.

In my mind's eye as I sit here typing this, I can see myself standing in front of a group of men as I have done so often, saying, "Cults take some portion of God's Word and rationalize it to justify their lifestyle, while the truth is that we are to make our lifestyle conform to God's Word."

That's why conversion is necessary to cure perversion. Homosexuals are prodigals like the rest of us, needing to "come home" to a loving Father. That's God's way.

Thinking of my former friends and how I had believed in them and trusted them, I sit here in the early hours of the morning trying to type with my eyes blurring with tears. I pray for each of them.

Odd as it may seem, even as I pray, I don't think I want to see them again. Not in their current milieu. Not to believe a lie again.

As I've said before, "It's easier to come out of the closet than to clean the closet." That's still true. Yet today gays want to insist that the closet is clean and that it's a matter of human rights to be homosexual. I agree with some of the great African American leaders today who are outraged by the homosexual's derailment of "human rights." As they put it, "I know plenty of homosexuals who are now straight, but I don't know any black man who is now white. It's not an issue of nature, but of choice."

I cannot close this chapter without saluting the many men I have met who faced their homosexuality, sought God with their entire being, and are now free of their former lifestyle. Some I know are now engaged in helping others to find their place in Christ.

The power of God is sufficient to the need.

There is no sin so great that God cannot forgive it.

There is no debt so large that God cannot pay it.

God's grace is sufficient.

So come home.

# CHAPTER FOURTEEN

## Know Your Enemy

There is a devil—he's the one who wants you to remain a prodigal—and his name is Satan. The reason so many do not recognize his presence in humanity is that he never comes as the devil, but as an angel of light. His every temptation first comes as an opportunity for good.

That's how Eve was deceived in the Garden of Eden. She saw that the tree was good for food, pleasant to the eyes, and something to be desired. Those are the three basic temptations: the lust of the flesh, the lust of the eyes, and the pride of life.[1] And, because she and Adam succumbed to them, the last Adam, the

Lord Jesus Christ, had to suffer the same three temptations on the mount and overcome them.[2]

When Jesus did that, He changed the very nature of temptation from an occasion of defeat to an opportunity for victory. From then until now, men with the Spirit of Christ can overcome their temptations—not in their own strength but in His.

Satan's temptation of Adam caused him to desire three things: to have what God had forbidden, to know what God had not revealed, and to be what God had not created him to be. Those are still man's three biggest desires when tempted.

Those aren't Satan's only approaches, however. I heard Dr. Paul Paino list eight ways the devil manifests his power:

1. In temptation to sin.
2. In accusation before God and the brethren.
3. By opposing the will and work of God.
4. By bringing confusion to truth.
5. Through idolatry and magic.
6. Through demon power.
7. Through many antichrists.
8. Through and by structural evils.[3]

Temptation is common to all. Sin occurs not when we're tempted, but when we're drawn to partake of it by our lusts.[4] Then lust conceives, gives birth to the sin, and the sin results in death.

———

From Eden until now, the devil has been accusing men before God, and God before men. He is called the "accuser."[5] Every time you hear someone accusing God, you know the source.

If we have believed in Jesus Christ as our Savior, however, Satan's accusations against us fall on deaf ears. I've heard it said, "The devil cannot win his case against you because Christ is your attorney." As the Bible puts it, "If anyone sins, we have an Advocate with the Father, Jesus Christ the righteous."[6]

Opposition was characteristic of the second year of Christ's ministry. Satan, the enemy of all righteousness, is diabolically opposed to anything divine. Remember that he's not God—he doesn't have God's nature or power. He's not omniscient, omnipresent, or omnipotent, though he would dearly love to be.

Immediately after the seed of God's Word is sown in the human heart, Satan comes to steal it away. In

Eden, he didn't attack Adam or Eve, but he attacked God's Word in which they believed, creating confusion in their minds. Satan will do the same to you.

The devil is the author of confusion, as well as lust. In the static powerlessness of confusion, when we find ourselves beset by uncertainty, evil can triumph. One of the most noted authors on war said, "A confused army leads to another's victory."[7]

Evil isn't just a matter of each of us being tempted as individuals. It can also be wrapped up in ideas or the guiding philosophies of organizations or governments. We call these "structural evils," such as organizations that are opposed to Christianity and biblical values and those that promote promiscuity and the abortion of unborn children.

Legalized gambling is another example. It is always presented as an opportunity for good to those who want to establish its presence in a state or community. It was proposed and accepted in two states where I lived, with the promise that it would help defray the costs of public education. However, in both cases, school taxes went *up* after it was legalized, not down, and all the money from gambling somehow never appeared to be used as was promised. And now it's an entrenched part of the American psyche.

Just recently, America considered a proposal for national health care, and its sponsors promised it would be good for all the people. When closely examined, however, the proposal took on the stature of a structural evil because of the way it would control and coerce citizens.

Even more frightening to many is the proposal for a national police force. Of course it's not called that, and it also is promoted as something good for the protection of the people. Germany fell for that line under Hitler.

Communism was advocated as an opportunity for all people to "share the wealth," but over the years it became a feudal system and a structural evil. Rather than setting people free as promised, it put them in bondage under political tyranny, and the wealth was shared only among the Communist Party bosses.

Condoms are presented as something good for those who are promiscuous, but instead they confuse the truth. The porous openings in a condom are 5 microns wide, but the HIV virus is only 0.1 microns wide.[8] What protection is that? The entire idea of condoms absolutely preventing disease is a lie. That lie protects a lifestyle, not people. And it's perpetrated by educators who cannot get students to turn in homework on time, yet expect them to control their lusts and use a condom.

When it comes to structural evil, though, there is probably no place as subject to it as the "high places" of the mind. Every prodigal problem takes root in the heart, but is created in thought. The mind is the battlefield of the heart.

When Jesus was tempted after His baptism, the diabolical "angel of light" wanted Jesus to reveal Himself as the Christ in self-centered miracles. Appearing at first to be good, such demonstrations would have been wrong—Satan's way rather than God's way.

When Adam sinned, he denied God's right of sovereignty, which exists by virtue of His being our Creator. God alone knows what's best for us, and His way is the greatest way. Turning our backs on that way, as revealed in His Word, can only do us harm.

Adam was created to be a son, not to be God. Satan's lie was based on a half-truth, and a half-truth is a whole lie. The temptation to partake of what was forbidden because it would make him and Eve "like God" is still the basis of every humanistic doctrine.

In Scripture, warfare and work go together. For instance, as the Israelites were rebuilding Jerusalem's walls under the direction of Nehemiah, we're told, "Those who built on the wall, and those who carried burdens, loaded themselves so that with one hand they worked at construction, and with the other held a weapon."[9] They knew who their enemy was. They were alert, and they were ready to fight whenever necessary.

We, likewise, must know our enemy, stay on the alert, and be ready to fight him every time he attacks. And our weapon? The same one Jesus used every time Satan tempted Him: "It is written . . ."—the truth of God's Word.[10]

Debt is also a structural evil. It always first appears as an opportunity for good—"Easy credit payment plans." Like all the devil's enticements, it promises to serve and please, but only enslaves and dominates. The debtor is not just a servant to the lender, but in too many cases he is a "slave."

Credit card debt is one of the major forms of indebtedness.

"Buy now—pay later." Sounds so good—but almost all such approaches for personal pleasure are based on usury by those offering it. Usury was prohibited by God in Israel's life, because it was a way of putting people in bondage or slavery.[11]

When the pleasure of sin is gone, the consequences can last for a lifetime or an eternity. Sin shows you only its pleasures, never its consequences. The same is true with debt. The consequences of inordinate debt can last for what seems like a lifetime.

Debt is a prodigal problem. It is incurred when we live apart from the ways of God, reject the Father's counsel in His Word, and do what we think is best for us.

Debt is also the devil's method to stifle the gospel. Charitable giving in America averaged 2.17 percent in a recent year; but, at the same time, credit card debt service averaged 19 percent. It was estimated that $46 billion was going to annual debt service on credit cards in the same year. What if we had given that interest payment to furthering the gospel instead?

All giving to God is predicated on how much of ourselves is given to God.

Living debt-free is liberty personified, while being in immoderate or exorbitant debt is servitude and enslavement. "Keep out of debt" is the injunction from God's Word.[12]

Whether personal or financial, freedom is God's pattern for our lives. Don't carry over your old patterns from your former life when you lived for the devil. Rely on the same power that gave you life in Christ to change your patterns of living. Change your thoughts by meditating on God's Word. Resist Satan's attacks on you personally, and resist his attacks on the Word of God that you believe.

# CHAPTER FIFTEEN

## Fathers!

To educate a man in mind and not in morals is to educate a menace to society," said President Teddy Roosevelt. One proof of that can be seen in the lives of some of the world's greatest philosophers of recent centuries. Those who were moral prodigals have done a great deal of damage to our world, and many of them had terrible relationships with their fathers.

Much of the insight in this chapter comes from Dr. Jess Moody, who made a study of the great philosophers. What he discovered is nothing less than astounding.

First, understand what philosophy is. It's a logical and critical study of the source and nature of human knowledge; a formal system of ideas based on such a study; and a basic theory about a particular subject or sphere of activity.[1]

Philosophy is basic for living either individually or collectively. It undergirds society. Every man has a philosophy by which he lives, no matter who, what, or where he is, how the philosophy was developed, or from whom it came.

According to Dr. Moody, there have been fifty-four great philosophers during the period covered from 645 B.C. until approximately 1960. Forty believed in God, and fourteen did not. Of the fourteen atheists, eight were preachers' sons.

Four of the atheists contributed mightily to the decline of the Western world. And those four shared fourteen identical characteristics. They all:

1. hated their fathers.
2. were heavily antifeminine.
3. were heavily anti-Christian.
4. were rabidly anti-Jewish.
5. had severe psychosomatic illnesses.

6. were repelled by human weakness.
7. were weak in mathematics.
8. had educational difficulties.
9. were sickly in the last quarter of their lives.
10. were depressive.
11. had exaggerated fears.
12. were extremely intolerant of opposition.
13. made exaggerated claims that were not true.
14. were suicidal.

Three of these four were Darwin, Freud, and Nietzsche, and each of these men wrote a book that influenced Hitler and Stalin. Those two men, in turn, were responsible for the deaths of fifty-seven million people in forty years.

Hitler hated his domineering father, a rabid atheist. Darwin's "survival of the fittest" doctrine was a great influence on Hitler, leading him to develop the philosophy of Aryan racial supremacy. Nietzsche's *Man and Superman* and Freud's *Moses and Monotheism* also influenced Hitler.

Stalin hated his father as well. Dr. Moody reports that Stalin and his mother danced in the streets when his father died.[2]

A chief characteristic of men who hate their fathers is that they usually adopt a surrogate father— someone to take the place of the despised. We find this same characteristic present today in young men who are "fatherless," who adopt a drug dealer or gang leader as a surrogate father. The dealers encourage and foster these relationships.

In Chicago, it was reported that gang leaders, drug dealers, and others "working the streets" buy the young boys shoes, jackets, and gold chains and give them money to further this substitute arrangement. Such an "adoption" process develops a strong bond and sets a pattern of behavior, as well as building a philosophy in the "son's" life.

Fatherless men are searching for fathers today. Many times in my own life, as I travel and minister, men have told me, "I never had a father, and through your books and tapes, you have become a father figure in my life."

Every son, through procreation, has a father, but he must have a father figure in his life for proper maturation. If his real dad isn't there, someone, somewhere, somehow will take his place. And, as in the cases of Hitler and Stalin, it often will not be a good substitute.

Something else occurs when sons hate their fathers: They tend to fail in school. Darwin did. It seems to be one way they have of embarrassing their fathers, getting revenge for their rejection, or vindicating their anger. The high drop-out rate in America's public schools today is probably directly related to the "fatherless" condition in the homes of so many kids.

Freud was a cocaine lover the first third of his career. He didn't believe it was addictive because the natives of South America used it for anesthesia when they were sick and for energy at work. When the news of his addiction was publicized, however, he lost his career.

I've always wondered how America became so addicted to drugs. Academia seemed to take to it, and the drug-using subculture of the baby boomers began on college campuses. When Freud's philosophical approach to life was so rabidly endorsed and accepted in those institutions of "higher learning," it seems they also endorsed his trait of loving drugs and passed it on along with his philosophy.

Today those same campuses are rife with anti-American philosophies, advanced by the same professors being paid by the country they dislike. How hypocritical! Decrying religion, denying God, the atheistic philosophy professor himself is a hypocrite.

Philosophy as a so-called science really can only ask questions; it can't provide any answers to the meaning of life. "Claiming to be wise, they became fools," is the way the Scripture describes the unrighteous.[3] They changed the glory of God into something they made to fit their own image.

God created man in His image, and ever since, men have been trying to return the favor. What do you suppose the world might be like today if Darwin, Freud, and Nietzsche had enjoyed good relationships with their fathers?

Judge Bob Downing in Baton Rouge, Louisiana, stated that almost 95 percent of the young defendants who come before his court or have been sent to prison from there admittedly hate their fathers.

Crime is a male problem. In Louisiana, there are 19,500 men in prison and only 500 women, and some man generally got each of the women in trouble.

The problem does not come from poverty, where they come from, or race—it's because they hate their father. They love their momma. Don't ever say anything about their momma or it's trouble. But the father was either not there, distant, or abusive.

I seldom see a young man in court who has a high school diploma, can name his pastor, and has a father at home who loves him.

Young men from middle—or upper-middle-class homes come before me, and I listen to their dads wonder aloud, "What happened?" They think they have given their sons everything—food, money, clothes, cars, put him in the best schools, played ball with him. . . .

The mother will say yes, we gave him everything. I took care of him, made sure he was in Sunday school, attended his sports events. . . .

And after I heard this over and over again, I started asking the fathers if *they* went to Sunday school or church with the family, and the answer was no. Dad stayed home and watched sports on TV, or went fishing or hunting. And, when the son got taller than Mom, he said, "If Dad can find God on TV or in the fishing boat or out hunting, then I can too." So, he's out the door.

Then he goes looking for a man he can look up to, and most of the time finds him in the wrong place. But the drug dealers and others know the son's need of a hero, buddy, or friend, and they determine it will be them.

We didn't have black-on-black crime years ago, when jobs were scarce and we didn't have running water. Why was that? Because Daddy was a deacon, Momma sang in the choir, and they were respected in the community.

Crack, the drug of choice, makes animals out of young men.

Not even an animal, though, would steal from its own parent. Crack addicts do. Railing against their grandparents for their Christian faith, pointing out their low-class status, faulting them for the lack of the "best things in life," they steal from them to support their habit, and then the grandparents mortgage that same home the grandson ridiculed to bail him out of jail.

## Fathers!

Those grandparents may not have had much, but they had their self-respect and the respect of their community. They were looked up to. People had regard for them.

Nobody knows who invented crack, the most addictive drug in society. Al Capone wouldn't steal from his mother, and even John Dillinger would not have taken his grandparents' Social Security check, yet a "crackhead" has no compunction about doing anything necessary to support his habit.

Putting people in jail is not the answer. People look to government to solve their problems. Government doesn't have a clue how to solve the drug problem. It just throws more money at the problem in prisons and treatment centers.

Only Jesus is the answer. I've seen many crackheads saved, give their lives to Jesus Christ, and be instantly healed of their addiction. It didn't take a 12-step or even a 30-day, $30,000 program to rehabilitate him. The government doesn't have to spend $35,000 a year to incarcerate him anymore.

When God restores a man to his family, He saves the whole family.

The last word from the prophet Malachi in the

Old Testament says that God will turn the hearts of the fathers to the children, and the children to the fathers. It doesn't say the mothers. Why? Because mothers take care of the children. It's only fathers who go off and leave the children.[4]

The son may stray from home, as I did, but he'll eventually come back as I did. Both my earthly father and my heavenly Father welcomed me back.

That's the way it was with the prodigal in Christ's parable. Leaving his father's house, he eventually was living in a pigsty (it could have been a crack house), and the pigs ate better than he did. He fed from the pods while the pigs ate the peas. No substance to his diet—just husks.

So it is with today's young men, brought into the world to reflect the glory of God but instead living on husks, nothing substantial in their lives, and subject only to concrete authority because they have never matured.

The "finer things in life" they hunger for are the virtues of real manhood—things that give dignity, worth, and value to a man. A man given to drugs is a fool. Here is what the book of Proverbs says concerning fools: "As a dog returns to his vomit, so a fool repeats his folly."[5] "The fool won't work and almost starves, but feels that it is better to be lazy and barely get by, than to work hard when, in the long run, it is all so futile."[6]

To be a good father, you must first learn to be a good son. But if you haven't had a good father helping to bring you through the process of maturation into the maturity of manhood, you'll have difficulty in becoming a good father yourself.

Because my dad wasn't a good father, I lacked qualities of real fatherhood in raising my own children. Fortunately, because of my relationship with God through Jesus Christ, His grace compensated for my lack, and my kids are great parents to their children.

My son, Paul, for example, is the dad of a lifetime for his children. His philosophy of fathering was developed in a godly home, where both parents loved each other, the family prayed and played together, and friends of the family lent a positive influence to their upbringing.

The philosophy of real Christianity will withstand the false ideologies and philosophies advocated in any school. Raised in the nurture and admonition of the Word of God, taught by the principles of righteousness, having a personal relationship with Jesus Christ, a son or daughter can withstand any onslaught of thought or doctrine.

Darwin, Freud, and Nietzsche, through their human philosophies, influenced Hitler and Stalin and brought death and desolation to the world in their generation. The apostles Paul, Peter, and John, through the philosophy of Jesus Christ, brought salvation, health, and life into the whole world.

Consider the results. Through Jesus Christ, believers are adopted into the family of God, and as good sons of God, are taught to be good earthly fathers.

My good friend John Binkley tells of the day when his blessings and prosperity began in earnest. It was while reading the Scriptures that the Word of God came alive to him, when he discovered that one of the commandments came with a promise from God: If you honor your father and your mother, the promise is long life.

John's parents were retired and living on a retirement income, and he had accepted their way of life without really thinking about it. After reading this principle, he began to study the condition of both his parents and the parents of his wife, Sharon. They both began to help support their parents, provide for them, help to make sure they were well taken care of, with their needs met.

Some time later when he began to wonder why he was having such good success, he traced it back to the time he made that decision. God honors us when we honor His Word. John's inadvertent negligence, when corrected, brought great favor and blessing.

Hatred of a father leads to rebellion and ruin. Repentance leads to reconciliation and restoration.

The hero of the parable is the Father, of course, who simply waited for the prodigal to grow up. We all have a heavenly Father, who, in great love for us, waits for us in our prodigal lifestyle to come to our senses and return to Him—to find again the inheritance we thought we had squandered.

Come on home.

# CHAPTER SIXTEEN
## The Culture of Christianity

Leaving South Africa, Zimbabwe, and Uganda, I flew to London, England, for some meetings. The people who assembled for the meetings in east London were themselves from Africa—Nigeria, Ghana, and Zambia. I was filled with wonder at what had happened in Africa and wanted to share it with the London people.

I began recounting how the first five books of the Bible were the stories of seven men. Though Eve sinned first, God gave the commandment to Adam, and God still holds the man accountable.

I spoke about the two Adams. The first Adam in

the Garden of Eden refused to accept responsibility for his actions, but the "last Adam," Jesus, accepted responsibility for the entire world. From one extreme, where man refused to accept any responsibility—for his actions or others'—to the other extreme, the Christlike man who accepts responsibility for the entire world for which Christ died. The more like Jesus, the more responsible a man becomes for others—to the laying down of his life for them.

Then, the second matter I laid before them was this principle: "If you have not proved faithful in that which belongs to another [whether God or man], who will give you that which is your own?"[1]

Facing those men, I reminded them that when they married, they married another man's daughter, and if they were not faithful in that which is another's, what makes them think they are qualified to have another man be faithful to their daughter? The teaching made an impact.

Thirdly, I taught the biblical truth concerning sex. This really got their attention. Scripture says, "Marriage is honorable among all, and the bed undefiled."[2] Only in marriage is the bed undefiled, and any sex outside of marriage is defiled because marriage is a covenant and sex is the sign of the covenant of marriage.

I told the men in London that as I went north from South Africa, the percentage of people infected with HIV grew greater nation by nation. In Uganda they told me 50 percent of the men had the virus. Probably that ratio was true with the men who came to hear me day after day.

"You only have one thing to give one time to one person in one lifetime!" I told single Ugandan men. "It's a gift so rare, so intrinsically valuable, so precious, so meaningful that God only gave one to each person. On the wedding night when you give her that gift and tell her it is something no other woman in the world will ever have, it belongs to her and her alone, then she knows she is God's gift to you and your gift to her is for a lifetime—the glory of your virginity."

When I left Africa the day before, flying on an airplane at 39,000 feet, I realized that if those three truths from God's Word would take hold of those hearing it, they contained the potential to halt the plague of AIDS on that continent. The realization so startled me that I wanted to tell it to the whole world. Education, government edict, and religion won't set you free. Truth will.

That evening in London when I finished teaching, as I made my way to the speaker's room, not a word was said to me—total silence. I finally asked the pastors what had happened. Had I done or said something wrong? One of the men spoke up and said, "We don't talk about sex to our people. We just thought promiscuity was part of our culture."

*Part of your culture?* I thought. *What culture? When you were born again, birthed into the kingdom of God, you were born into a new culture!*

Culture defines a civilization. It is a particular form of civilization, beliefs, customs, language, art, music, and institutions of a society at a given time.[3] So says the dictionary.

When you are born again and enter into the kingdom of God by being birthed in and of the Holy Spirit, you become a citizen of a heavenly civilization, in which the government rests upon the shoulders of Jesus Christ. It is based on the moral law of love that Christ established with His new covenant.

The Sermon on the Mount is to the new covenant

what the Ten Commandments were to the old. Jesus took the Mosaic Law and established it and fulfilled it. Then He took the moral, ceremonial, and judicial elements of it and issued a new "moral law of love" as the standard for the New Covenant.

"Jesus said unto him, 'Thou shalt love the Lord thy God with all thy heart, and with all thy soul, and with all thy mind. This is the first and great commandment. And the second is like unto it, Thou shall love thy neighbor as thyself. On these two commandments hang all the law and the prophets.'"[4]

Jesus raised the level of life from the earthly to the heavenly, from the flesh to the spirit. He made it a matter of the heart—a condition of faith, not works.

The law says if you hate someone enough to kill them, but never do, you are not guilty of murder. Christ's new covenant of the moral law of love says if you thought it in your heart, you're guilty! The old law says if you lust after a woman to commit adultery, but don't do it, you are not guilty. However, the moral law of love says it was in your heart to do it, therefore—guilty!

It is impossible to live on the level of the moral law of love except by the power of the Spirit of Christ.

It's impossible to human nature. Only with the new nature that Christ gives is it possible. This is the reason we must be indwelt by His Spirit to live in His kingdom.

I was born into the culture of America and have lived my life according to those distinguishing features of it. I grew up in, and lived my life in, its civilization.

However, when I was born into the kingdom of God, I entered into a new culture and have spent my life since then enjoying the glory of it. Just as I was taught the ways of my earthly culture, so have I spent a lifetime in the Word of God, which is the "constitution" of this new civilization, so I would know how to live in it.

I am a Christian living in America. I live in a culture within a culture. Many times I am faced with a culture clash, but the heavenly is greater than the earthly. If I seek first the kingdom of God, then all other things will be added.[5]

Christianity is not a subculture in a country, but a counterculture. It is counter to the ways of the world. Its standard is higher, and those who are earthly are frustrated because they cannot see the virtue in it.

Having lived in the world's culture and then being born into the culture of Christianity, a Christian can understand how the world operates—how the worldly think and what the worldly are doing—but the world cannot understand the Christian culture because it is only spiritually discerned. Understanding must come by revelation, not by explanation.

Genuine Christianity is lived on a higher moral level than the immoral or legal level most of the world lives on, but it's when Christians descend to the unbelievers' level that the world castigates and condemns Christianity.

There is a paradox in all this. Society accepts the aberrant behavior of the non-Christian as "normal," but the actions of Christians are viewed as "abnormal." The Bible shows that sin is abnormal, and Christianity is normal. God created man to live normally—in fellowship with Him, but sin brought the abnormality of separation.

Another paradox is in the truth about light and dark. In the natural world, those in the light cannot see into darkness, while those in the dark can see clearly what is in the light. Yet walking in the light of Christ, a believer can see clearly what is happening in the moral darkness of this world, though those in the world cannot "see" the light.

My answer to the pastors in London is that promiscuity is not part of the Christian culture. Nor are other ways of the flesh and sin. They don't mix.

The prodigal mistook the culture of a foreign land to be better than that of the Father's house. He learned his lesson the hard way. Most prodigals do.

There is a better way: "Walk in the Spirit, and you shall not fulfill the lust of the flesh."[6]

Converted? *Yes!*

Cultured? *Yes!*

# CHAPTER SEVENTEEN
## The Way Home

You want everybody to think you've got four aces, when all you're holding is a pair of deuces. That's how the prodigal was. Where do you start to get back to the Father? Go to the Father's house!

"The way of the Cross leads home," is more than a lyric to a Christian hymn.[1] It's where you find the Father. It's where the Father sent His only begotten Son to meet with us. It's where Jesus came in His righteousness to be identified with our sin, so we could come in our sin to become identified with His righteousness.

The Cross is the one and only place where we can be assured that God will meet with us and make the exchange. Blood was shed there. A life was given. It was a place of exchange where earth and heaven met, so hell would be robbed of its prey. It's the only place where a prodigal is assured of a "Welcome home."

Once when Jesus was ministering to His disciples, He asked them a question: "Who do people say that I am?"[2] They gave Him various opinions that people held: "Elijah," "Elisha," "one of the prophets."

"But, who do you say that I am?" He asked.

"Thou art the Christ, the Son of the living God," Peter answered.[3]

Jesus commended Peter and told him that this revelation did not come from natural sources, but from the Spirit of God. Jesus continued talking, telling them He must go to Jerusalem, suffer many things, be crucified, and be raised on the third day.[4]

As He was talking, Peter, who had just been commended for the answer he gave Jesus, must have felt a sense of importance, because he took Jesus aside and rebuked Him. "God forbid, Lord! This must never happen to You," he told Jesus in no uncertain terms.[5]

Jesus answered him, "Get thee behind me Satan! You are in my way, for you are minding what partakes not of the nature and quality of God, but of men."[6] Smarting from the rebuff and rebuke himself, Peter fell silent while Jesus went on to tell His disciples what it meant to be His disciple. "If you would be my disciple, take up your cross and follow me."[7]

It was His way of telling Peter that not only would He, the Son of Man, suffer the Cross, but all who followed Him would need to suffer their own cross. The Cross to Jesus meant not doing what He willed or wanted but what the Father sent Him to do. The will of the Father was what the Cross meant to Him; it meant more than life itself.

So, the disciples learned their lesson. If doing the will of God does not mean more than personal life or death, then it doesn't mean enough. Life and death are what it cost Jesus, and are the cost to those who would be His disciples.

Not all disciples will die as He did, but all will have to die. Death to those who follow Him means death to self. Primarily and fundamentally Jesus said, "Whoever confesses Me before men, him I will also confess before My Father who is in heaven. But whoever denies Me before men, him I will also deny before My Father who is in heaven."[8]

To confess Jesus publicly before men is to have your identity swallowed up in His, or to lose your identity in Him. Until you mention His name, you have your own identity, but once your mention Him—His identity supersedes yours. You lose your identity in His.

The place where that initial exchange takes place is at the Cross. It is there that you confess your sin, ask forgiveness, believe, and rely entirely on what Christ did at Calvary to make an atonement for your sin. It is there that God becomes identified with you. Jesus' blood is applied to your sin, His Spirit enters your heart, your mind is renewed, and you are spiritually transformed into the kingdom of God.

Your testimony to others of what has happened in your life identifies you with Him. The Cross is where the prodigal comes home, is forgiven, and is given a new life. It's where repentance is converted to faith, and salvation for eternity takes place. It's where the prodigal is treated like a prince.

When Peter rebuked Jesus for telling of His crucifixion, Jesus, in turn, called Peter "Satan." It was not because Peter had become infected with a diabolic virus, nor because the devil suddenly had possession of him. It was because Peter sounded like the devil.

When the first Adam succumbed to temptation in the Garden of Eden, it became an occasion of defeat for humanity. Remember, to change the nature and character of temptation from the negative force it was to a positive opportunity for victory in our lives, Jesus had to suffer the same temptations and overcome them.

The apostle John wrote that "all" that is in the world is the "lust of the flesh, the lust of the eyes, and the pride of life."[9] Every temptation in human life comes from one of those three. Adam and Eve succumbed to them in the garden. Jesus went up on the mountain to meet them.

After forty day of fasting, the devil appeared with the same temptations to which Adam and Eve had submitted, but Jesus resisted the devil through the power of God's Word, and having overcome them, returned in the "power of the Spirit." Now, those of us who are in Christ also overcome through the Spirit of Christ that dwells in us. It changes each of us from a prodigal to a prince.

One of the temptations Jesus suffered was Satan's offering to give Him all the kingdoms of this world if He would only bow down and acknowledge Satan. Actually, Satan wanted Jesus to "worship" him.

When Satan was an archangel in heaven, then called Lucifer, he became "lifted up with pride," and wanted to take the place of God.[10] Rather than lead worship, he wanted to be worshiped. The sin of sedition started there. Satan is the progenitor of lust, and sedition is just one characteristic of lust.

Jesus was worth "all the kingdoms of this world."[11] It was part of His inheritance by going to the Cross. By omitting the Cross, Satan would retain his power. But by Jesus' going to the Cross, it would cancel Satan's power.

Peter telling Jesus that He did not need to go to the Cross sounded like something from the devil, or a philosophy of proud and sinful men, inspired by Satan.

To omit the Cross in Christianity makes Christianity to be no more than any other religion on the face of this earth. No other god, prophet, philosopher, guru, or religious zealot ever did what Christ did—die for the sins of men. That's why Christianity is unique in all the earth.

Jesus knew: No Cross—no crown. He knew: No death—no resurrection. That's why every prodigal must come home to the Father by way of the Cross.

The Cross is where Christ laid down His life for us and where we lay down our life for His. Life-enhancement Christians want the life without the Cross. Can't be done. To try to be a Christian without any Cross is to become an enemy of the Cross—and of God.

Once we as prodigals come to the Cross, what does it mean to "take up the cross"? Simply to put the will of God first and foremost in our lives. Loving God more than we love our own lives. Making the Word of God the sole source of our faith and the absolute rule of our conduct.

William Tyndale loved God and the Word of God. His love affair was shown in his devotion to translate the Bible into the English language so the common man could read it for himself. When it was done, he was called a heretic and convicted by his peers. He was strangled by a hangman, then burned at the stake.

Three years after Tyndale's death, there was a Bible in every church in England. Tyndale loved Jesus more than life itself.

Nine years later in England, John Cranmer, Archbishop of Canterbury, and John Rogers, who edited *Matthew's Bible*, were burned at the stake by the queen known as "Bloody Mary." Four years after their deaths, another queen reinstated that Bible in the church.

Men fought and died for the right to read the Bible—while today's prodigal preachers say they "would rather preach about starvation or justice than those silly Bible stories." Those who make such statements have never been to the Cross. They don't have a clue what it means, nor that the Cross is the only place where eternal life is gained.

No prodigal ever found his way back to the Father unless he was willing to go by way of the Cross.

Neither will you.

# CHAPTER EIGHTEEN
## Establishing New Patterns

Bryce was in the military when he married. He was every inch the marine, from the top of his crew cut to the spit and polish on his shoes. He loved his life in the service of his country, and sometimes his wife wondered whether he even loved it more than he loved her.

Habits, training, and discipline learned in the military are not the same as those in marriage. Many men in close-contact careers are abusive to their wives because of the violent nature of their professions.

In communicating at home, Bryce was operating

on a military "need to know" basis, which is good for the military, but not for a wife. "Yes, sir" and "No, sir," may be fine when addressing an officer, but it is not exactly pillow talk. "Reliable communication permits progress," is the principle found in Proverbs.[1] Bryce had to embark on establishing new speech patterns for his home life. He started to give his wife details, and he perfected the art of listening. The new patterns were necessary for right living. The change in patterns brought a change in relationship.

Failure is the womb of success. "Yesterday's dung is tomorrow's fertilizer." Men take what they learn from failure and use it for the platform on which to build a new, successful venture. Present success erases past failure. Do you want to overcome all the false starts and failures of your past? Be successful. The greatest antidote to failure is success. You can do it.

God is a specialist at taking what was meant for evil, turning it around, and making it work for our good.[2] It's in the very nature of His transcendent glory. It is His good pleasure to give us the kingdom. He paid the price at Calvary for us to have it. He delights in our having it.

## Establishing New Patterns

So many men fear failure. Yet, if men never failed, there would be no need of a Savior. We are all prodigals in need of someone to save us from ourselves, as well as from sin. When God installed the first Adam in the Garden of Eden, God made it pleasant and obedience was easy.

God created Adam without a sinful nature, put him in an ideal environment, provided all temporal needs, endowed him with strong mental powers, gave him a life partner to complete him, and gave him duties to engage his mind and body. Above all, God established a personal father-son relationship between Adam and Himself.

Adam's rupture of that relationship came from an internal desire that produced an external action. The externals in life always begin with the internals. God warned him of the consequences of disobedience. Still, Adam chose self over God, and his disobedience resulted in expulsion from Eden, a symbol of his separation from God and His kingdom. Adam became a prodigal whose progeny were destined to depravity, and man is totally incapable of changing this nature of his. Only God can transform human nature.

Adam now lived under the judgment of his own actions.

Punishment proceeds from justice and is not intended to reform the offender. Chastisement proceeds from love and is intended for correction. Chastisement by God is for the purpose of education, instruction, training, corrective guidance, and discipline.

When law demands the infliction of punishment, it is a just retribution, not a means to an end. Therefore, a release or forgiveness of the penalty is needed, such as a pardon. However, God cannot pardon the sinner simply on the basis of his repentance. God can only pardon when the penalty for sin is first paid.

God is able to forgive the sinner when he repents because Christ paid the penalty for sin. Pardon for sin was already accomplished in Him, and man can be forgiven and reckoned righteous before God.

Repentance is not an apology for mistakes, but a genuine desire to admit sin, forsake the wrong, and turn to embrace the right. It is not a satisfaction rendered to God, but a condition of the heart necessary before we can believe unto salvation. Saving faith cannot operate in a man's heart until repentance takes place. When we repent and receive salvation, we go from being a prodigal to a pauper to a prince.

Birthed as a "new creation" into a "new culture" means being educated, disciplined, refined, and readied for a "new inheritance." The prodigal had originally been born and educated in his Father's house, but in his wasted years, he developed habits of mind, body, and soul that needed to be undone in order to again be the heir of his house. Our pattern of living, so destructive in self-willed lifestyle, must be changed to fit our new lifestyle and heritage. It is vital that we begin to make God's ways our ways, because His ways are as far above ours as the heavens are above the earth.[3] Ours are naturally of the flesh; His are supernaturally of the Spirit.

Patterns we established in prodigal living need to be changed once we are back in the Father's house. Old ways need to be exchanged for new ones. Thought patterns we learned in prodigal living need to be brought under the Spirit's control to live acceptably in the Father's house. Without the change, the old patterns will destroy the new life in Christ.

Such change requires radical action. The prophet Jeremiah talked about it in describing God's divine direction in his life. "See, I have this day set you over the nations . . . To root out and to pull down, / To destroy and to throw down, / To build and to plant."[4] Before God plants and builds what He wants, it is first necessary to get rid of the existing structure. That's the pattern for constructing a new life when you leave prodigal living.

I'll never forget a minister friend, Campbell McAlpine, recounting Bible history as an example to illustrate this very truth. He was teaching how the Hebrew children who came out of Egypt were not allowed to enter Canaan because of their unbelief. Refusing to believe God's Word that Canaan was the land of promise, God said they were calling Him a liar and slandering the land. For this, the entire generation that came out of Egypt died before the children of Israel entered the land of Canaan. Campbell said that every morning Moses would find Joshua and ask how many had died the previous day, and when Joshua told him, Moses would reply, "Thank God, we're getting closer."

The moral of this story is this: The more of our old

patterns and ways that drop off of us, the closer we are to being where God wants us to be. Breaking the failure cycle is one of life's greatest accomplishments.

Change your ways. You do it by reading the Word constantly, praying, and acting in obedience to what God tells you. The anointing of God's Spirit not only "breaks the yoke" of sin but is vital to avoid a relapse into old patterns. No man can flee from himself. As with the prodigal, he can only run to the Father to be free from his past.

Restlessness issuing from sin does not let the conscience rest. Its torment is more than an absence of peace, it is a condition of burning memory—a fire that cannot be quenched apart from the forgiveness of the Father's love.

"He who guilelessly puts away sin by repentance will surely find that God lovingly puts it away with pardon."[5] With the absolution of sin, there is entire and complete acquittal. Guilt is gone. Peace at last.

If we walk in princely power, following patterns set by our heavenly Father, life becomes sweet. What was only dreamed of in the days of worldly pleasure, now becomes a reality when living by the pleasure of God. Self-pleasing is never as wonderful as God-pleasing. "It is your Father's good pleasure to give you the kingdom," is what God's Son said about our Father.[6]

Mathematics is based on addition, subtraction, division, and multiplication. Each can be either positive or negative. Subtracting old ways, adding new patterns in light of truth, while eliminating divisions and strife, and multiplying the blessings make a good life. The pattern Christ gives is like a yoke that is easy and a burden that is light.[7] You choose the pattern you will wear.

The prodigal in the parable developed a pattern of pleasurable living, without either responsibility or accountability, but he met concrete authority when he found himself without friends, family, food, or money. There was only one place to go—back to the father.

Dividing himself from his father, yoked to his insubordination, caused a subtraction of his inheritance, added the burden of poverty, and multiplied his sorrows.

It works both ways.

Subtracting his opposition to his father's will by repentance, adding right thinking, dividing himself from the foreign land, and returning home brought a multiplication of blessings.

God's math is basic.

The choice is yours.

Add. Subtract. Multiply. Divide.

Will it be prodigal, pauper—or prince?

"Give me" or "Make me?" Two words can change your eternity.

# CONCLUSION

- Grow up.
- Take responsibility.
- Think before you act.
- Order your daily life according to God's Word.
- Invest yourself in relationships more than in "things" that can never satisfy.
- Use things like time and money, don't let them use you.
- Seek God's mercy.
- Be a good father.
- Pattern yourself after your God-given role model: Jesus Christ.
- Manhood and Christlikeness are synonymous.
- Never forget there is a powerful enemy who wants to destroy you, but He who is for you is greater—infinitely more powerful and wise—than any enemy.

- Whenever you act like a prodigal, run to your Father God.
- Repentance and faith must be balanced. You can't have one without the other.
- Don't forget; you're only young once, but you can live immaturely for a lifetime.
- Act like a man!

These are some of the actions and principles of a maximized man.

Is it easy to be a maximized man? No way! Never has been. Never will be. But maximized manhood is the way to lasting, fulfilling relationships with God, your wife, your children, your neighbors, your coworkers, your world. It's the way of integrity. It's the way to be a credible witness of Jesus Christ to the world around you, influencing others for eternity.

Now, more than ever, our world needs maximized men. It's the way I want to live. It's the life I enjoy. More than ever, it's all I want to be.

How about you?

# NOTES

## Introduction

1. Luke 15:11–24 paraphrase

## Chapter One

1. Prov. 3:15–18

## Chapter Two

1. Ps. 55:21 AMPLIFIED BIBLE
2. Paraphrased from *Webster's New Collegiate Dictionary* (Springfield, MA: G & C Merriam Co., 1976).
3. Gal. 5:19
4. Prov. 14:9 TLB
5. Eccl. 4:13 KJV
6. Luke 9:48 TLB
7. See Luke 7:47 TLB.

## Chapter Three

1. Gen. 3:12
2. Jer. 6:14 TLB
3. Jer. 51:30
4. Jer. 51:30
5. 1 Cor. 13:11
6. Luke 7:31–32
7. 1 Cor. 14:20 KJV

## Chapter Five

1. *Maximized Manhood* back cover (Springdale, PA: Whitaker House, 1982).
2. Dale Carnegie, *How to Win Friends and Influence People,* revised edition (New York: Pocket Books, 1981), 211, 223.
3. Luke 16:31
4. Matt. 11:21; Matt. 10:15
5. 1 John 1:9
6. *Maximized Manhood,* 142.
7. Dr. Jess C. Moody, tape series, "Darwin's Children and Nietzsche's Nephew" (Porter Ranch, CA: Shepherd of the Hills Church).
8. Patrick F. Fagan, "The Real Root Cause of

Violent Crime: The Breakdown of the Family,"
*The Indian Life Magazine*, May—June 1986, vol.
18, issue 2, 5.

9. "State of the Union as Clinton Reports to
Congress, Citizens Are Busy Remaking
America," *Time*, 30 January 1995, 36.

10. Mal. 4:6

## Chapter Six

1. Ps. 37:1 KJV

2. 1 Tim. 5:8

3. 1 Cor. 9:16

4. Matt. 28:19

5. Paul E. Tan, "One Historic Vote," *Encyclopedia
of 77,000 Illustrations* (Rockville, MD:
Assurance Publishers, 1985), 620.

## Chapter Seven

1. *Journal of Essential Documents in America*,
1997, 1.

2. Josh. 24:15

3. Judg. 2:10 KJV

4. James 4:4

5. Ray Comfort, *Hell's Best Kept Secret* (Springdale, PA: Whitaker House, 1989), 10–11.
6. John 16:33; 14:22; Rom. 8:35
7. Acts 4:12 KJV
8. 1 Thess. 1:10; Rom. 5:9
9. James 1:2
10. Gal. 6:14

## Chapter Eight
1. Eph. 5:25
2. Jer. 1:12 KJV

## Chapter Nine
1. Rom. 13:8 AMPLIFIED BIBLE
2. Prov. 22:7

## Chapter Ten
1. Matt. 19:8
2. Heb. 13:4 KJV

## Chapter Eleven
1. James 2:13

2. Heb. 4:12
3. James 2:13
4. James 4:2
5. Lam. 3:22

## Chapter Twelve

1. Eccl. 3:1
2. Edwin Cole, *Strong Men in Tough Times* (Orlando, FL: Creation House, 1993), 21.
3. Eph. 5:33
4. Eph. 5:21
5. Matt. 6:20

## Chapter Thirteen

1. Gen. 13–19
2. Acts 15:20, 29

## Chapter Fourteen

1. 1 John 2:16
2. Matt. 4
3. Seminar by Pastor Paul Paino.
4. James 1:14–15
5. Rev. 12:10

6. 1 John 2:1
7 Su Tzu, *The Art of War*, trans. Samuel B. Griffin (London: Oxford University Press, 1963), 82.
8. Center for Disease Control, Atlanta, GA.
9. Neh. 4:17
10. Matt. 4:4, 7, 10
11. Deut. 23:19–20; Ex. 22:25
12. Rom. 13:8

## Chapter Fifteen

1. *Webster's New Collegiate Dictionary*
2. Moody, "Darwin's Children."
3. Rom. 1:22 AMPLIFIED BIBLE
4. Judge Bob Downing, audiotape testimony, Baton Rouge men's event, Christian Men's Network, 1995.
5. Prov. 26:11 TLB
6. Eccl. 4:5–6 TLB

## Chapter Sixteen

1. Luke 16:12 AMPLIFIED BIBLE
2. Heb. 13:4
3. *Webster's New Collegiate Dictionary*

4. Matt. 22:37–40 KJV
5. Matt. 6:33
6. Gal. 5:16

## Chapter Seventeen

1. Jessie Pounds and Charles Gabriel, "The Way of the Cross." Copyright 1969 Gospel Publishing House.
2. Paraphrased from Matt. 16:13
3. Matt. 16:16; Mark 8:25 KJV
4. Matt. 16:21
5. Matt. 16:22; Mark 8:32
6. Matt. 16:23; Mark 8:33
7 Matt. 16:24 paraphrase
8. Matt. 10:32–33
9. 1 John 2:16
10. Isa. 14:11–15
11. Matt. 4:8

## Chapter Eighteen

1. Prov. 13:17 TLB
2. Gen. 50:20
3. Isa. 55:9

# Notes

4. Jer. 1:10
5. Isa. 55:7
6. Luke 12:32
7. Matt. 11:30